# A SYLLABUS FOR
# HOLY LIVING

Julius Gilbert White

**Remnant Publications, Inc.**

Copyright © 2006
**Remnant Publications, Inc.**

Printed in the USA

Published by
Remnant Publications, Inc.
649 E. Chicago Rd.
Coldwater, MI 49036
www.remnantpublications.com

Cover Design by Penny Hall
Text Design by Greg Solie – Altamont Graphics

# —— CONTENTS ——

# —— INTRODUCTION ——

I n this great climactic hour of the great controversy, we find the world and all its institutions trembling under the crushing load of sin. Moreover, we find ourselves now standing on the very edge of chaos.

Despite our mental acknowledgment, we find ourselves—the remnant church—too much and too often asleep—asleep in the carnal security of the Laodicean condition, not understanding (or just refusing to act upon) the ominous signs of the approaching destruction.

Yes, today as never before, a possible nuclear holocaust rears its ugly head on the horizon of a world terrified by the humanly uncontrollable forces of political, military, and economic strife. Soon, very soon, Jesus must come or sinful man will destroy the world and the entire human race

"And the nations were angry, and thy wrath is come, and the time of the dead, that they should be judged, and that thou shouldest give reward unto thy servants the prophets, and to the saints, and them that fear thy name, small and great; and shouldest destroy them which destroy the earth" (Revelation 11:18).

In *Testimonies*, vol. 6, 14, we read from Inspiration the description of today's world: "We are standing upon the threshold of great and solemn events. Prophecies are fulfilling. Strange, eventful history is being recorded in the books of heaven. Everything in our world is in agitation. There are wars and rumors of wars. The nations are angry, and the time of the dead has come, that they should be judged. Events are changing to bring about the day of God, which hasteth greatly. Only a moment of time, as it were, yet remains. But while already nation is rising against nation, and kingdom against kingdom, there is not now a general engagement. As yet the four winds are held until the servants of God shall be sealed in their foreheads. Then the powers of earth will marshal their forces for the last great battle."

The material in this book will help you understand the urgency of our time, and how to prepare to meet the coming crisis of the little time of trouble, the sealing, and the latter rain. Most importantly, it will help you understand the reality of victory over sin through the

5

power of the Holy Spirit, and how to share this experience with everyone you meet. The end will come suddenly, unexpectedly, as an overwhelming surprise to the world and to the Seventh-day Adventist Church (see *Testimonies* vol. 8, 28, 37; *Seventh-day Adventist Bible Commentary,* vol. 7, 989).

"For when they shall say, Peace and safety; then sudden destruction cometh upon them, as travail upon a woman with child; and they shall not escape. But ye, brethren, are not in darkness, that that day should overtake you as a thief. Ye are all the children of light, and the children of the day: we are not of the night, nor of darkness. Therefore let us not sleep, as do others; but let us watch and be sober. For they that sleep sleep in the night; and they that be drunken are drunken in the night. But let us, who are of the day, be sober, putting on the breastplate of faith and love; and for an helmet, the hope of salvation" (1 Thessalonians 5:3-8).

Let us wrench ourselves from our passiveness, indifference, and spiritual death. Let us no longer sleep as do others, but watch and be sober.

The Publishers

# — ONE —
# A Perfect Character the Goal

God has devised a redemption plan and provided ways and means possessed of infinite resources and power to meet every great and minute need for changing men and women back into the perfect likeness of His own character.

However, human experience, as recorded in Holy Writ and as seen today, indicates that man is prone to doubt that it can be done, or to become confused in his idea *how to receive* the provisions of the gospel, and let them operate in his life for his perfect transformation.

Man's own experience has always been his greatest problem. How shall he relate himself to his Maker so that the provisions of the gospel shall operate within him?

What is the experience through which a sinner is to pass by which he becomes again a child of God, receives the divine nature, becomes like God in character, and is saved in the kingdom of heaven? How shall man receive the power of God to enable him to live a holy life?

These are the greatest questions in the world—the greatest questions man can ask—and the problem involved is the greatest which has confronted mankind in all ages.

To reach this goal should be the first aim of life of all people—members of all religious faiths—but more especially those who are looking for Christ to soon return and raise the righteous dead and translate the living saints who have gained the victory over all sin. They have the hope in their hearts of experiencing that grand climax to the operation of the plan of redemption for six thousand years (see 1 Corinthians 15:52–54; Revelation 22:14, 14:12; 2 Peter 3:14; 1 John 3:1–3). A few comments on these texts follow:

"The characters formed in this life will determine the future destiny. When Christ shall come, He will not change the character of any individual. Precious, probationary time is given to be improved in washing our robes of character and making them white in the blood of the Lamb. To remove the stains of sin requires the work of a lifetime. Every day renewed efforts in restraining and denying self are needed. Every day there are new battles to fight and victories to be gained. Every day the soul should be called out in

7

earnest pleading with God for the mighty victories of the cross" (*Testimonies*, vol. 4, 429).

"We believe without a doubt that Christ is soon coming. This is not a fable to us; it is a reality. We have no doubt, neither have we had a doubt for years, that the doctrines we hold today are present truth, and that we are nearing the judgment. We are preparing to meet Him who, escorted by a retinue of holy angels, is to appear in the clouds of heaven to give the faithful and just the finishing touch of immortality. When He comes, He is not to cleanse us of our sins, to remove from us the defects in our characters, or to cure us of the infirmities of our tempers and dispositions. If wrought for us at all, this work will all be accomplished before that time. When the Lord comes, those who are holy will be holy still. Those who have preserved their bodies and spirits in holiness, in sanctification and honor, will then receive the finishing touch of immortality. But those who are unjust, unsanctified, and filthy, will remain so forever. No work will then be done for them to remove their defects and give them holy characters. The Refiner does not then sit to pursue His refining process and remove their sins and their corruption. This is all to be done in these hours of probation. It is now that this work is to be accomplished for us" (*Ibid.*, vol. 2, 355).

"It is a solemn thing to die, but a far more solemn thing to live. Every thought and word and deed of our lives will meet us again. What we make of ourselves in probationary time, that we must remain to all eternity. Death brings dissolution to the body, but makes no change in the character. The coming of Christ does not change our characters; it only fixes them forever beyond all change" (*Ibid.*, vol. 5, 466).

The attainment of this goal—victory over all sin—is the purpose of every doctrine of the Bible, from the simplest truth to the greatest line of prophecy. Every Bible truth has but one object—to lead the believer through an experience which will restore the image of God in his soul and perfect his character.

Some religionists attempt to simplify it by saying, "Only believe on the Lord Jesus Christ and thou shalt be saved," which is true; but their interpretation of what it is to "believe" is so narrow and perverted that they eliminate the necessity of keeping the law of God, and so they abolish law and make the work of the gospel all a work of what they term "grace." They are teaching only a part of Christian experience.

Other religionists quote the same text, and although they teach the observance of the law—the entire Ten Commandments—their interpretation of what it is to "believe" is likewise such that the correct relation between "faith" and "works" is not set forth; and so, while they are a step nearer the truth than those first mentioned but stop short of the full truth, they do their followers a greater harm in teaching it as the whole truth, for the greater the proportion of truth, and the smaller the proportion of error mixed together, the more deceptive and dangerous it is. The message concerning Christ's second coming in this generation has summed up all Bible truth into one grand last message, and is directed at Christian experience to produce perfect characters and a perfect church.

The call of the message sounding in all the world is, "Come out of her, my people," and "Keep the commandments of God." To those who contemplate joining this movement and preparing for the end of all things, the keeping of the commandments of God is a great test. Many never join because they deem it impossible. Some people stumble over the possibility of keeping the fourth commandment, the outward physical observance of the Sabbath. Some surrender to God and decide to keep His holy day, and to them He makes its observance possible.

The Advent movement is composed of people who have entered into this experience of surrender to God and obedience to His commandments. However, after they are within the movement they find themselves confronted with the problem of *perfect obedience* to all of the commandments—with the problem of victory over the last sin as the preparation for translation—and this becomes the *supreme test of their experience.* This is the great test of the faith of God's last church. Many struggle along, and not finding the way to do it, give it up in discouragement. Some continue struggling, hoping that somehow the way will yet be found. Others are continually advancing in their experience and daily drawing nearer the coveted goal. For nigh six thousand years Satan has held that God is asking the impossible and therefore is unjust.

Now if God be God indeed, He is not requiring the impossible; it is possible for the gospel to do its work; His plans are not imperfect, but will work successfully if they are followed. This brings us directly to the study of the daily experience the Christian is to have to conquer sin and perfect holiness.

## God's Plan For Christian Experience

A key text for this treatise, one which sounds a very encouraging note, is found in Proverbs 4:18, A.S.V. "The path of the righteous is as the dawning light, that shineth more and more unto the perfect day."

This cheering conception of Christian experience as a growing thing has been set in beautiful verse as follows:

"The light of the world shines brighter and brighter
As wider and wider God opens my eyes;
My trials and burdens seem lighter and lighter,
And fairer and fairer the heavenly prize.

"The wealth of this world seems poorer and poorer
As farther and farther it fades from my sight;
The prize of my calling seems surer and surer
As straighter and straighter I walk in the light.

"My waiting on Jesus seems dearer and dearer
As longer and longer I lean on His breast;
Without Him I'm nothing, seems clearer and clearer,
As more and more sweetly I lean on His breast.

"My joy in my Saviour is growing and growing,
And stronger and stronger I trust in His Word
My peace like a river is flowing and flowing
As harder and harder I lean on the Lord."

                                                    —*Selected*

Second Peter 1:5–11 also explains the progression of the experience in the things of God by the application and use of divine principles, and states with great clearness the certainty of success if God's plan is followed: "And beside this, giving all diligence, add to your faith virtue; and to virtue knowledge; and to knowledge temperance; and to temperance patience; and to patience godliness; and to godliness brotherly kindness; and to brotherly kindness charity. For if these things be in you, and abound, they make you that ye shall neither be barren nor unfruitful in the knowledge of our Lord Jesus Christ. But he that lacketh these things is blind, and cannot see afar off, and hath forgotten that he was purged from his old sins. Wherefore the rather, brethren, give diligence to make your calling and election sure: for if ye do these things, ye shall never fall: for so an entrance shall be ministered unto you abundantly into the everlasting kingdom of our Lord and Saviour Jesus Christ."

## The Gospel of Grace Operates According to Laws

All of God's work of "grace" is done according to unvarying laws which are systematized into a science.

"There are great laws that govern the world of nature, and spiritual things are controlled by principles equally certain. The means for an end must be employed, if the desired results are to be attained" (*Testimonies,* vol. 9,221).

## Character Not by a Miracle

"The prophets and apostles did not perfect Christian character by a miracle. They used the means which God had placed within their reach; and all who put forth the effort will reach the same result" (*The Sanctified Life,* 84).

"There is a science of Christianity to be mastered, a science as much deeper, broader, higher, than any human science as the heavens are higher than the earth. The mind is to be disciplined, educated, trained; for men are to do service for God in ways that are not in harmony with inborn inclination. Often the training and education of a lifetime must be discarded, that one may become a learner in the school of Christ. The heart must be educated to become steadfast in God. Old and young are to form habits of thought that will enable them to resist temptation. They must learn to look upward. The principles of the Word of God, principles that are as high as heaven and that compass eternity, are to be understood in their bearing on the daily life. Every act, every word, every thought, is to be in accord with these principles. No other science is equal to that which develops in the life of the student the character of God" (*Counsels to Parents, Teachers, and Students*, 20).

## The Simplicity of the Science of Salvation

A simple way to approach the study of human experience in receiving divine principles is to study one principle at a time and how it works to change the heart.

Christian experience may, for this purpose, be separated into its primary essentials as a ray of light may be separated into its seven primary colors. These essentials may be likened to a ladder of seven rounds let down from heaven for man to grasp by faith and use under the influence and direction of the Holy Spirit, in his advancement toward the kingdom of heaven (No special stress is laid on the order in which these are named).

# — TWO —

# Prayer
## *The First Essential*

### Visiting with the Infinite

In the beginning men did not pray; Adam talked with God face to face. After sin brought its guilt, "no man can see Him and live" (*Early Writings*, 122). Sin has separated the creature from the Creator, but even so, we may still visit with Him though He is unseen. Prayer brings us back by faith into the audience chamber of the Infinite One:

### — Unseen But Not Unknown —

Jesus, these eyes have never seen
That radiant form of Thine;
The veil of sense hangs dark between
Thy blessed face and mine.

I see Thee not, I hear Thee not,
Yet Thou art oft with me;
And earth has ne'er so dear a spot
As where I meet with Thee.

Like some bright dream that comes unsought,
When slumbers o'er me roll,
Thine image ever fills my thought,
And charms my ravished soul.

Yet tho' I have not seen, and still
Must rest in faith alone,
I love Thee, dearest Lord, and will,
Unseen, but not unknown.

*—Ray Palmer*

Prayer may be called the first round of the ladder toward heaven, for prayer lies at the very foundation of experience in divine things.

"Prayer is the key in the hand of faith to unlock heaven's storehouse" (*Steps to Christ*, 94).

Prayer is the gateway to the throne of the great God of the universe.

Prayer is the means God has given us to use by which we shall receive everything in the gospel.

"Ask, and it shall be given you; seek, and ye shall find; knock, and it shall be opened unto you; for every one that asketh receiveth; and he that seeketh findeth; and to him that knocketh it shall be opened. Or what man is there of you, whom if his son ask bread, will he give him a stone? Or if he ask a fish, will he give him a serpent? If ye then, being evil, know how to give good gifts unto your children, how much more shall your Father which is in heaven give good things to them that ask him?" (Matthew 7:7–11).

"It is a part of God's plan to grant us, in answer to the prayer of faith, that which He would not bestow did we not thus ask" (*The Great Controversy,* 525).

Every Christian knows that the more we pray the stronger we are:

> Lord, what a change within us one short hour
> Spent in Thy presence will prevail to make.
> What heavy burdens from our bosoms take.
> What parched grounds revive as with a shower.
> We kneel, and all around us seems to lower;
> We rise, and all the distant and the near
> Stands forth in sunny outline, brave and clear.
> We kneel, how weak! We rise, how full of power!
>
> Why, therefore, should we do ourselves this wrong
> Or others, that we are not always strong;
> That we should ever weak or heartless be,
> That we are ever overcome with care,
> Anxious or troubled, when with us is prayer,
> And joy, and strength, and courage are with Thee!
> —*Archbishop Trench*

## How Shall We Go to God?

How shall we go to Him in prayer? With what spirit shall we go, and what shall be our attitude toward Him? We must sense something of who He is; that He is as much greater, higher, and purer than we, as the heavens are higher than the earth. He is the great Creator! He is both mighty and perfect! "Holy and reverend is his name" (Psalm 111:9).

We are lost sinners, worms of the dust. We must not rush into or out of His presence. We must go with reverence and awe, with humility, submission, surrender, and confession. We must acknowledge our sin. We are to use no vain repetitions, but to pray with the simplicity of a broken heart.

## For What Shall We Pray?

We are to pray to God for pardon, for correction and guidance; for His viewpoint of every question, for His ideas of life, for His ideals, plans, and purposes for our lives and affairs, and then for power to execute His will thus sought and revealed.

We are to pray for His attributes and character to be imparted to us. In short, we go to God to be *changed* more than to get things. If we seek for things instead of seeking for God, *they become our idols:*

### — My Prayer —
Not for peace, and not for power;
Not for joy, and not for light;
Not for truth and not for knowledge,
Not for courage in the fight;
Not for strength to do Thee service
Not for these my prayer shall be;
Not for any gifts or graces,
But for Thee, Lord, just for Thee.

Make me lonely for Thy presence
Every earthly friend above;
Make me thirst for Thine indwelling;
Make me hungry for Thy love,
Till in full and free surrender,
I shall yield my life to Thee;
Only then in full perfection
Canst Thou give Thyself to me.

All the beauty that I seek for,
Every treasure I would own
Thou art these in rich completeness;
They are found in Thee alone.
All the loveliness I long for,
All the best that I would be,
I can never find them elsewhere
Than in Thee, Lord, just in Thee.

Empty me of all my glory,
All my boasting, all my pride;
Let my righteousness, my wisdom,

On Thy cross be crucified;
Fill me, then, with all Thy fullness,
All Thy will work Thou in me;
In Thyself is nothing lacking;
Make me, Lord, complete in Thee.
                              —*Annie Johnson Flint*

Matthew 6:33 makes it plain that seeking after righteousness must take precedence over seeking after mere things.

We are to ask only for the things that will make us and others more like God—things that will be used in doing His will. "Ye ask and receive not, because ye ask amiss, that ye may spend it in your pleasures" (James 4:3, A.S.V.).

"Whatever we receive must be used in doing His *will*" (*Education,* 258).

When the prodigal left home (Luke 15:12, 19) he said to his father, "Give me," but when he returned he changed his plea to "Make me." "Prayer is not to work any change in God; it is to bring us into harmony with God" (*Christ's Object Lessons,* 143). "Prayer is the opening of the heart to God as to a friend. Not that it is necessary in order to make known to God what we are, but in order to enable us to receive Him. Prayer does not bring God down to us, but brings us up to Him" (*Steps to Christ,* 93).

We are not to try to persuade God to give us what we want, but we are to seek after His desires for us—after the things He wants to give to us, and the things He wants to do for us and wants us to do.

## Surrender

All of this means that we are to go to Him in perfect surrender, with absolute submission to Him. This thought was crystallized into one little phrase which Jesus put into "The Lord's Prayer" when He said, "Thy will be done."

The grave danger of going to God with even a coveted idea unsurrendered is told in Ezekiel 14:1–11.

## Communion in Prayer

We should not rush into God's presence, neither should we hurry away, but tarry and let Him speak to us. "They that wait upon the LORD shall renew their strength" (Isaiah 40:31). It was when Moses went to speak to God that God spoke to him (see Numbers 7:89). The communion of prayer is its most precious feature. In other words, more good is obtained from God's speaking to us than from our talking to Him. We cannot tell Him anything He needs to know, but He can tell us everything we need to know.

"Many, even in their seasons of devotion, fail of receiving the blessing of real communion with God. They are in too great haste. With hurried steps they press through the circle of Christ's loving presence, pausing perhaps a moment within the sacred precincts, but not waiting for counsel. They have no time to remain with the divine Teacher. With their burdens they return to their work.

"These workers can never attain the highest success until they learn the secret of strength. They must give themselves time to think, to pray, to wait upon God for a renewal of physical, mental, and spiritual power. They need the uplifting influence of His Spirit. Receiving this, they will be quickened by fresh life. The wearied frame and tired brain will be refreshed, the burdened heart will be lightened.

"Not a pause for a moment in His presence, but personal contact with Christ, to sit down in companionship with Him, this is our need" (*Education*, 260, 261).

While we are waiting and listening, our hearts are impressible and His Spirit is able to make impressions upon our hearts, bring His Word to our minds, refresh our memories, and impart new thoughts to us.

Such communion helps us to sense that we are in His very presence while in prayer, and also that we live in His presence always. Being in His presence lessens the desire to sin.

There is a sense in which we may commune with God in all places and under all circumstances, and so the apostle wrote, "Pray without ceasing" (1 Thessalonians 5:17). Jesus said, "Men ought always to pray" (Luke 18:1).

There are many hindrances to being always in a prayerful frame of mind with our thoughts turned heavenward. These hindrances must be put away and overcome.

"In order that we may be kept by the power of God through faith, the desires of the mind should be continually ascending in silent prayer. When we are surrounded by influences calculated to lead us away from God, our petitions for help and strength must be unwearied. Unless this is so, we shall never be successful in breaking down pride and overcoming the power of temptation to sinful indulgences which keep us from the Saviour" (*The Youth's Instructor*, August 18, 1898).

"They cannot be constantly on their knees, but they can be uplifting their hearts to God. This is the way that Enoch walked with God" (*Testimonies*, vol. 5, 596).

One poet has beautifully explained how anyone may always pray anywhere:

"There is a viewless, cloistered room,
As high as heaven, as fair as day,
Where, though my feet may join the throng,
My soul may enter in and pray.

"One hearkening, even, cannot know
When I have crossed the threshold o'er;
For He alone, who hears my prayer,
Has heard the shutting of the door."
—Selected

Mother, who is perhaps the busiest person in the world, tells how she prays without taking any extra time, and how it sanctifies her work, and makes her more faithful to do it well:

## — Time Enough to Pray —
The while she darns her children's socks,
She prays for little stumbling feet;
Each folded pair within the box
Fits faith's bright sandals, sure and fleet.

While washing out with mother pains
Small dusty suits and frocks and slips,
She prays that God may cleanse the stains
From little hearts and hands and lips.

And when she breaks the fragrant bread,
Or pours each portion in its cup,
For grace to keep their spirits fed
Her mother-heart is lifted up.

O busy ones, whose souls grow faint,
Whose tasks seem longer than the day,
It doesn't take a cloistered saint
To find a little time to pray.
—*Ruby Weyburn Tobiss*

When we really learn to pray, the fellowship with God as we commune with Him becomes the sweetest joy of life:

Alone with Thee,
O God, my soul would be
I seek this calm retreat,
This quiet hour to meet
Alone with Thee.

No deeper joy than this
Can come to me.
I do not see Thy face,
Yet in this holy place
Faith findeth Thee.

I do not hear Thy voice;
I speak to Thee,
And in my heart is heard
An answer from thy word
To comfort me.

Adoring throngs in heaven
Surround Thy throne;
There Thou to them art near and
Thou, O God, are here,
With me alone.
—*Robert F. Gordon*

Thus we are to live the life of prayer; to pray about everything, and to keep the heart always lifted to God in prayer. This will contribute mightily to victory.

"Communion with God through prayer develops the mental and moral faculties, and the spiritual powers strengthen as we cultivate thoughts upon spiritual things" (*The Desire of Ages*, 70, 71).

## Family Prayer

Family prayer protects its members from sin, but too often it is neglected. "In every Christian home God should be honored by the morning and the evening sacrifices of prayer and praise. Children should be taught to respect and reverence the hour of prayer. It is the duty of Christian parents, morning and evening, by earnest prayer and persevering faith, to make a hedge about their children.

"In the church and at home the children are to learn to pray and to trust in God. Teach them to repeat God's law. Concerning the commandments the Israelites were instructed: 'Thou shalt teach them diligently unto thy children, and shalt talk to them when thou sittest in thine house, and when thou walkest by the way, and when thou liest down, and when thou risest up' (Deuteronomy 6:7). Come in humility, with a heart full of tenderness, and with a sense of the temptations and dangers before yourselves and your children; by faith bind them to the altar, entreating for them the care of the Lord. Train the children to offer their simple words of prayer. Tell them that God delights to have them call upon Him.

"Will the Lord of heaven pass by such homes and leave no blessing there? Nay, verily. Ministering angels will guard the children who are thus dedicated to God. They hear the offering of praise and the prayer of faith, and they bear the petitions to Him who ministers in the sanctuary for His people, and offers His merits in their behalf" (*Counsels to Parents, Teachers, and Students*, 110).

## Neglect Not Prayer

"In too many households prayer is neglected. Parents feel that they have no time for morning and evening worship. They cannot spare a few moments to be spent in thanksgiving to God for His abundant mercies—for the blessed sunshine and the showers of rain, which cause vegetation to flourish, and for the guardianship of holy angels. They have no time to offer prayer for divine help and guidance and for the abiding presence of Jesus in the household. They go forth to labor as the ox or the horse goes, without one thought of God or heaven. They have souls so precious that rather than permit them to be hopelessly lost, the Son of God gave His life to ransom them; but they have little more appreciation of His great goodness than have the beasts that perish" (*Patriarchs and Prophets*, 143, 144).

## No Substitute for Prayer

Prayer is a precious gift of Heaven. By it God imparts His gifts of grace for our salvation, but *we must use it or these blessings will not come to us* though provided in infinite plenitude.

One reason we find salvation in such meager measure is that we pray so little.

Heaven has no substitute for prayer. If we fail to use this means of grace there is no other way of receiving it; we must suffer the loss, and the loss will be eternal. Jesus is our Example in prayer as well as in all other matters. Will you make fuller use of prayer in the future?

Your destiny is in your own hands.

# —— THREE ——
# Faith
## *The Second Essential*

F aith is the second round in the divine ladder of experience by which the Christian rises in triumph over every obstacle, —rises in victory and toward Heaven. It is used in connection with prayer and with every act and experience of life. Without it prayer is mockery, valueless. "Prayer is the key in the hand of faith to unlock heaven's storehouse, where are treasured the boundless resources of Omnipotence" (*Steps to Christ*, 94–95).

## What Is Faith and How Used?

1. Faith is to believe that God is (see Hebrews 11:6).

2. It is to believe what He says (see Romans 10:17).

Before we can believe what He says we must know what He says. This means that we need a wide knowledge of the Bible. The more we know of His Word the larger basis we have for faith, the wider field for the operation of faith, and the stronger will our faith be. It naturally grows while we read His Words.

3. We must act in harmony with what He says (see Luke 6:10; Matthew 4:22; Matthew 17:27).

4. We must make our requests in harmony with what He has said in harmony with His promises and their conditions.

"Genuine faith has its foundation in the promises and provisions of the Scriptures" (*The Desire of Ages*, 126). "Faith comes by the Word of God" (*Ibid.*, 429).

"Faith is the assent of man's understanding to God's Words" (*Review and Herald*, December 1, 1904).

"The foundation of all true faith is the Word of God, for faith comes by hearing, and hearing by the Word of God. Anything which does not have the Word of God as its foundation is not true faith" (*Review and Herald*, June 12, 1924).

5. We must trust in God to take care of all the consequences of doing what He has said (see Matthew 14:26–33).

"Christ's ambassadors have nothing to do with consequences. They must perform their duty and leave results with God" (*The Great Controversy,* 609, 610).

The purest faith believes implicitly in what God has said even when we cannot see how it can be true. It believes God will take care of the consequences when we cannot see any way through. God Himself is out of sight; many of His ways of working are out of our sight, and are revealed only when we come to our extremity and have shown that we absolutely believe Him. Examples—the opening of the Red Sea for Israel; His command to the sick to walk; to Peter to walk on the water; and to look in the mouth of the fish for money.

Faith, then, is our belief and confidence in Him and His *promises,* not in our prayers, but in that which inspires our prayers. Therefore, before we pray we ought to look in the Bible and the Testimonies of His Spirit to see what God has said about the matters concerning which we wish to pray, and then we should *ask according to what He has said,* surrender everything in the life that is contrary to His Words, and com*ply* with every condition He has specified. Then we can believe He will answer according to His Word, and we can trust in His *promise—not* in our *prayer.*

"We do not trust in our finite prayers, but in the Word of our Heavenly Father" (*Review and Herald,* November 19, 1895).

"Many who are sincerely seeking for holiness of heart and purity of life seem perplexed and discouraged. They are constantly looking to themselves, and lamenting their lack of faith: and because they have no faith, they feel that they cannot claim the blessing of God. These persons mistake feeling for faith. They look above the simplicity of true faith, and thus bring darkness upon their souls. They should turn the mind from self to dwell upon the mercy and goodness of God and to recount His promises, and then simply believe that He will fulfill His Word. We are not to trust in our faith, but in the promises of God" (*The Sanctified Life,* 89).

"God stands back of every promise He has made. With your Bible in your hands say, I have done as Thou hast said. I present Thy promise, 'Ask, and it shall be given you; seek, and ye shall find; knock, and it shall be opened unto you' [Matthew 7:7]" (*Christ's Object Lessons,* 147).

## Presumption

One kind of presumption believes God will answer because we ask, rather than because He has promised. Another kind presumes He will answer even though we have not searched for and complied with all the conditions He has given.

## God's Favorite Promises

| | |
|---|---|
| Forgive | 1 John 1:9—Confess, forgive |
| if | Isaiah 1: 18—Though your sins be as scarlet |
| repent: | Isaiah 40:1–2—Forgive double |
| confess | Romans 5:20—Pardon much greater than the sin |
| obey | Matthew 6:12—Christ so teaches us |
| Give | Romans 1:16—The gospel is the power |
| power | Isaiah 40:28–31—Power to the faint |
| to | Philippians 4:13—Christ strengthens us |
| obey | 2 Corinthians 12:9—His strength made perfect in our weakness |
| Give | James 1:5–8—Wisdom if not waiver-settled |
| wisdom | Psalm 25:9—Meek guide with judgment if use it to His glory. |

## Troublesome Texts

Matthew 9:29—"According to your faith be it unto you." See that your "faith" is based upon a promise of God, and is not merely a belief that He will answer because you ask, and this text presents no problem.

Mark 11:20–24—"When ye pray, believe that ye receive them, and ye shall have them." However, the request must be based upon a promise, and must be in harmony with His will or it will not be granted. He will not give merely because we ask when our request is contrary to His expressed will. This is made very plain in the following:

"Christ says, 'What things soever ye desire, when ye pray, believe that ye receive them, and ye shall have them' (Mark 11:24). He makes it plain that our asking must be according to God's will; we must ask for the things He has promised, and whatever we receive must be used in doing His will. The conditions met, the promise is unequivocal" (*Education*, 257, 258).

Many people read the promise, "When ye pray, believe that ye receive them, and ye shall have them"—and conclude that anything may be had if we only believe that God will give that for which we ask. They say, "If we have faith enough," and so they try to believe strongly enough to obtain the things which they request. Such a course would place in human hands the decision of what God shall grant and what He shall withhold. Such decisions God has never committed to humanity. That would be foolish. Were that the case any Christian would pray for a million dollars; for the conversion of all the heathen without so much toil and sacrifice; for the conversion of all the people in our respective cities, and of all our relatives; that he might never die; that all the sick be healed, and so on without end. However, such is not the case. The keystone of the arch of prayer must always be, *"Thy will be done"* (Matthew 26:42)—absolute surrender of every possession, plan, ambition, idea, thought, and power, and this surrender must be renewed and made more complete every day:

## — Thy Will Be Done —

"Yesterday, when I said, 'Thy will be done,'
I knew not what that will of Thine would be,
What clouds would gather black across my sun,
What storms and desolation waited me;
I knew Thy love would give me what was best,
And I am glad I could not know the rest.

" 'Thy will be done,' I say, and to the scroll
Of unread years consenting, set my name;
Day after day their pages will unroll
In shining words that prove Thy love the same,
Until my years are gathered into one
Eternal, sanctified, 'Thy will be done.' "

—Selected

# — FOUR —
# Living by Faith

Section 3 was "The Prayer of Faith," which might be called the first phase of "Righteousness by Faith." This section is "Living by Faith," the second phase of "Righteousness by Faith"—the relation between "faith" and "works."

The text for this section is, "The just shall live by faith" (Romans 1:17; Hebrews 10:38).

The thought in "living by faith" is not that of living a faith, for it cannot be made a substitute for money or food or any material thing; the thought is that we are to live *according to* faith. If faith is based upon the Word of God, then it is but another way of saying that we are to live according to the Word of God, and so it is. Faith comes from the Word of God (see Romans 10:14), and we are to live according to every Word of God (see Matthew 4:4). Therefore, before doing anything we should *see what God has said about it—and* then *do as He has said.* That is living by His Words, and that is living by faith in what He has said. One can eat by faith by eating the food God has specified; dress by faith by wearing such attire as God has said becomes His children; marry by faith by marrying "only in the Lord" as He has said; and so on with everything in life.

## The Application

Each individual should know what God has said about the experiences he is having and about the work he is doing, and should act accordingly.

Explicit instruction has been given in the Bible and the Testimonies concerning the life and work of the gospel minister. He should know this instruction and follow it. That will be to live by faith and minister to the needs of humanity by faith. The same principles apply to those in official positions of all kinds throughout the work of God, and to the physician, nurse, local elder, deacon and all church officers, Sabbath-school officers and teachers, church school boards and Young People's society officers, to the parent and youth and child, and all lay members—everybody.

The same principle applies to all methods of labor and procedure, all plans of organization and operation of the work, home missions, foreign missions; evangelical, educational and publishing operations; to tithing and making offerings; to the sale of literature and Ingathering and Bible work; to our contacts with the world in recreation and amusements, in labor unions, secret societies and life insurance; to matters of attire in dress, hair, jewelry, wedding rings, and so forth; to our everyday health habits and the food we eat; to the kind of reading we choose, the sort of conversation we hold, the associates we choose, and the marriage unions we make. God has given detailed instruction covering every work and every experience of each individual or worker. To *know* this instruction and then to *follow* it is to *live by faith*. True it is that oft times we cannot see why God has required or forbidden this or that, or what will be the consequences of doing as He has said, but faith accepts that which *cannot be seen*.

To ignore His will on any point, take liberties with what He has said and follow our own desires and then pray for Him to bless us, is presumption.

A very broad application of these great principles summed up concerning one truth is this: If we believe that Christ is coming soon, we will live as if we expected to see Him; we will be faithful even unto death we can die by faith if need be even as we can live by faith.

Thus the entire life should be lived by faith; not in an ecstasy of trust that rests in God's hands *waiting for Him to do* all these things, but a life of *active endeavor to do everything* just as He has commanded. Every act of life should be based upon the instruction God has given. We are to work and pray, and then believe that God will remove every mountain of difficulty that is in the way and make it possible for us to do all He has specified.

Thus faith works, as is set forth in James 2:14–26.

## How to Increase Our Faith

Faith is based on something God has said in His Word. If we read and believe one thing He has said, we have one degree of faith. If we read another promise or word of instruction and believe that, we now have two degrees of faith. When we read and believe ten of His promises we have ten degrees of faith. We can add to our measure of faith any time we wish to do so by reading more of His Word. We can have all the faith we want; go to the Word and help ourselves to it like we do to fresh air or water. God inspires faith in our hearts as we read His Words.

## Examples of Faith (See Hebrews 11)

- Hebrews 11:1 and Romans 10:17—Faith is assurance based upon a promise. The fulfillment is involved in the promise though they are "things not seen."
- 11:2—By it "the elders obtained a good report."
- 11:3—By faith we understand that Creation was performed by the Word of God—our faith in the Word of God teaches us that truth.
- 11:4—By faith Abel offered a sacrifice according to the Word of God—he acted by faith.
- 11:5—"By faith Enoch was translated," because "he pleased God"—he did what God said he ought to do for three hundred years.
- 11:6—If we come to God we must (a) believe that He is, and (b) believe He will do what He says He will do.
- 11:7— "By faith Noah" did what God said.
- 11:8—"By faith Abraham … obeyed," not knowing what would come of it.
- 11:9—"By faith" Abraham sojourned, and his family also.
- 11:10—By faith he looked for the city.
- 11:11—"Through faith" Sarah conceived seed and "judged him faithful who had promised."
- 11:12—By faith a multitude sprang from one believing one promise.
- 11:13—"In faith" these died, still believing the promise.
- 11:14—Thus they manifested their faith.
- 11:15—They could have turned back, but they would not.
- 11:16—They desired a better country. "God is not ashamed" of them, and "has prepared for them a city."
- 11:17—"By faith Abraham" … offered up Isaac.
- 11:18—Who was his only hope.
- 11:19—He believed God could bring him back.
- 11:20—"By faith Isaac blessed."
- 11:21—"By faith Jacob" … blessed.
- 11:22—"By faith Joseph" commanded that his bones be taken back to Canaan.

- 11:23—"By faith Moses" was hid by his parents
- 11:24—"By faith Moses" refused the throne of Egypt.
- 11:25—By faith Moses chose suffering rather than prosperity.
- 11:26—And counted "reproach of Christ" greater than riches.
- 11:27—"By faith" Moses left Egypt.
- 11:28—"Through faith" Moses kept the Passover.
- 11:29—"By faith they passed through the Red Sea."
- 11:30—"By faith the walls of Jericho fell."
- 11:31—"By faith ... Rahab perished not."
- 11:32—How many more examples of what faith is (action based upon a command or promise of God) do you need?
- 11:33–38—What "faith" caused people to do.
- 11:39—Those only received the promise of salvation, not it's fulfillment.
- 11:40—They are still waiting for us. [They are not yet in heaven.]
- 12:1—They are a "great cloud of witnesses" who have left us many beautiful examples to follow. Let us put aside every thing that hinders our doing so, and let us run—make haste to know and to do the will of God.
- 12:2—"Looking unto Jesus."

## Righteousness by Faith
## Faith and Obedience Go Together

"While God can be just, and yet justify the sinner through the merits of Christ, no man can cover his soul with the garments of Christ's righteousness while practicing known sins, or neglecting known duties. God requires the entire surrender of the heart, before justification can take place; and in order for man to retain justification, there must be continual obedience, through active, living faith that works by love and purifies the *soul*" (*Review and Herald,* November 4, 1890).

### Faith and Presumption

The following extract is taken from a wonderful chapter on faith, all of which should be read in this connection:

"True faith and true prayer, how strong they are! They are as two arms by which the human suppliant lays hold upon the power of Infinite Love. Faith is trusting in God—believing that He loves us, and knows what is for our best good. Thus, instead of our own way, it leads us to choose His way. In place of our ignorance, it accepts His wisdom; in place of our weakness, His strength; in place of our sinfulness, His righteousness. Our lives, ourselves, are already His; faith acknowledges His ownership, and accepts its blessing. Truth, uprightness, purity, are pointed out as secrets of life's success. It is faith that puts us in possession of these. Every good impulse or aspiration is the gift of God; faith receives from God the life that alone can produce true growth and efficiency.

"Faith is not feeling. 'Faith is the substance of things hoped for, the evidence of things not seen' (Hebrews 11:1). True faith is in no sense allied to presumption. Only he who has true faith is secure against presumption, for presumption is Satan's counterfeit of faith.

"Faith claims God's promises, and brings forth fruit in obedience. Presumption also claims the promises, but uses them as Satan did, to excuse transgression. Faith would have led our first parents to trust the love of God and to obey His commands. Presumption led them to transgress His law, believing that His great love would save them from the consequences of their sin. It is not faith that claims the favor of Heaven without complying with the conditions on which mercy is to be granted. Genuine faith has its foundation in the promises and provisions of the Scriptures.

"To talk of religion in a casual way, to pray without soul-hunger and living faith, avails nothing. A nominal faith in Christ, which accepts Him merely as the Saviour of the world, can never bring healing to the soul. The faith that is unto salvation is not a mere intellectual assent to the truth. He who waits for entire knowledge before he will exercise faith, cannot receive blessing from God.

"It is not enough to believe about Christ; we must believe in Him. The only faith that will benefit us is that which embraces Him as a personal Saviour; which appropriates His merits to ourselves. Many hold faith as an opinion. But saving faith is a transaction, by which those who receive Christ join themselves in covenant relation with God. Genuine faith is life. A living faith means an increase of vigor, a confiding trust, by which the soul becomes a conquering power" (*Gospel Workers*, 259–261).

"Angels of God will preserve His people while they walk in the path of duty, but there is no assurance of such protection for those who deliberately venture upon Satan's ground" (*Testimonies*, vol. 5, 198).

"You are on the enemy's ground. You have voluntarily placed yourself there, and the Lord will not protect you against his assaults" (*Ibid.*, 436).

## Presumption to Go Where Error Is Taught

He who is conscious that he has been blessed with much knowledge of truth should beware of going to listen to those who have less light than he, or who are teaching a mixture of truth and error, unless he has business there. By doing so he turns from a *great light* to a *lesser* light and voluntarily places himself in the *dusk,* under the influence of error, which gives the enemy of his soul an advantage over him. To expect that God will send angels to protect him there, is *presumption.* We should ever press toward the light and seek for an increase of light.

## How to Use Faith

The chapter entitled "Faith and Prayer" in the book, *Education,* should be read at this point in this study. In it is found this forceful statement:

"How to exercise faith should be made very plain. To every promise of God there are conditions. If we are willing to do His will, all His strength is ours. Whatever gift He promises, is in the promise itself. 'The seed is the word of God' (Luke 8:11). As surely as the oak is in the acorn, so surely is the gift of God in His promise. If we receive the promise, we have the gift.

"Faith that enables us to receive God's gifts is itself a gift, of which some measure is imparted to every human being. It grows as exercised in appropriating the Word of God. In order to strengthen faith, we must often bring it in contact with the Word. …

"Through faith in Christ, every deficiency of character may be supplied, every defilement cleansed, every fault corrected, every excellence developed" (*Education*, 257).

## Faith and Works

Many Christians are sadly confused concerning the relation of faith to works; some, even to the point of believing that obedience is not necessary if we have the right faith. Yet the matter is as simple as this:

If I accept what God has said about how I should take care of my body which He made in His image and wishes to use as His temple, it of necessity follows that I will do as He has said; this produces "works" which are performed because of the faith I have in Him and what He said. *Faith causes action;* in other words, *faith works.* Thus it is with everything in life.

When I do that which He asks me to do because He asks it, to do so is not my own "works," but is an act of faith; I do it because I

29

believe in Him. Furthermore, I also believe He is with me in performing such acts and adds His strength to my effort. When I believe that His strength is present to make up for my weakness, He makes it so. That also is of faith.

Very plain, helpful thoughts will be found in the following counsel concerning this point.

## God and Man Cooperate

"If we are faithful in doing our part, in cooperating with Him, God will work through us the good pleasure of His will. But God cannot work through us if we make no effort. If we gain eternal life, we must work, and work earnestly. ... The characters we form here will decide our eternal destiny. ... Our part is to put away sin, to seek with determination for perfection of character. As we thus work, God cooperates with us, fitting us for a place in His kingdom. ... The doing of God's will is essential if we would have an increased knowledge of Him. Let us not be deceived by the oft-repeated assertion, 'All you have to do is to believe.' Faith and works are two oars which we must use equally if we press our way up the stream against the current of unbelief. 'Faith, if it hath not works, is dead, being alone' (James 2:17). The Christian is a man of thought and practice. His faith fixes its roots firmly in Christ. By faith and good works he keeps his spirituality strong and healthy, and his spiritual strength increases as he strives to work the works of God" (*Review and Herald*, June 11, 1901).

"When, through faith in Jesus Christ, man does according to the very best of his ability, and seeks to keep the way of the Lord by obedience to the Ten Commandments, the perfection of Christ is imputed to cover the transgression of the repenting and obedient soul" (*Fundamentals of Christian Education*, 135).

"True success in any line of work is not the result of chance or accident or destiny. It is the outworking of God's providences, the reward of faith and discretion, of virtue and perseverance. Fine mental qualities and a high moral tone are not the result of accident. God gives opportunities; success depends upon the use made of them.

"While God was working in Daniel and his companions 'to will and to do of his good pleasure' (Philippians 2:13), they were working out their own salvation. Herein is revealed the outworking of the divine principle of cooperation, without which no true success can be attained. Human effort avails nothing without divine power, and without human endeavor, divine effort is with many of no avail. To make God's grace our own, we must act our part. His grace is given to work in us to will and to do, but never as a substitute for our effort" (*Prophets and Kings*, 486, 487).

## The Right Kind of Faith

"A mere profession of discipleship is of no value. The faith in Christ which saves the soul is not what it is represented to be by many. 'Believe, believe,' they say, 'and you need not keep the law.' But a belief that does not lead to obedience is presumption. The apostle John says, 'He that saith, I know him, and keepeth not his commandments, is a liar, and the truth is not in him' (1 John 2:4). Obedience is the test of discipleship. It is the keeping of the commandments that proves the sincerity of our professions of love. When the doctrine we accept kills sin in the heart, purifies the soul from defilement, bears fruit unto holiness, we may know that it is the truth of God. When benevolence, kindness, tender-heartedness, sympathy, are manifested in our lives; when the joy of right-doing is in our hearts; when we exalt Christ, and not self, we may know that our faith is of the right order" (*Thoughts from The Mount of Blessing*, 146, 147).

## Not Authority But for Godlikeness

"God requires obedience, not for the purpose of showing His authority, but that we may become one with Him in character. We will find in God the attributes of character needed to form characters after His likeness. We are to form characters that are in harmony with the Deity. Thus our natures become spiritualized in every faculty" (*The Upward Look*, 347).

## Faith and Reason

"The Word of the Lord, spoken through His servants, is received by many with questionings and fears. And many will defer their obedience to the warning and reproofs given, waiting till every shadow of uncertainty is removed from their minds. The unbelief that demands perfect knowledge will never yield to the evidence that God is pleased to give. He requires of His people faith that rests upon the weight of evidence, not upon perfect knowledge. Those followers of Christ who accept the light that God sends them must obey the voice of God speaking to them when there are many other voices crying out against it. It requires discernment to distinguish the voice of God.

"Those who will not act when the Lord calls upon them, but who wait for more certain evidence and more favorable opportunities, will walk in darkness, for the light will be withdrawn. The evidence given one day, if rejected, may never be repeated" (*Testimonies,* vol. 3, 258).

"Through faith we understand that the worlds were framed by the Word of God, so that things which are seen were not made of things which do appear" (Hebrews 11:3).

"Why does the apostle introduce the thought of Creation thus early in the study of faith? He has already shown that faith is stronger than hope. He wishes now to contrast faith with *reason,* and so he brings in something which, if grasped at all, must be accepted by faith and not worked out by reason. Think of it! A void, empty space; God speaks, and out of nothingness there springs into existence a world clothed in beauty and filled with living creatures. That is a fact which must and can be accepted only by faith. Faith works in a field beyond reason. Reason, improperly used, is faith's worst enemy, and such use of reason has destroyed many a man's faith.

"Reason is the eye of the mind. Someone makes a statement to you and you say, 'I cannot see that.' Then the person begins to explain and reason with you, and presently you say, 'Oh, I see it now.' What do you mean? You mean that your reason has grasped it, and it is now a matter of mental sight.

"But you may ask, 'Does reason have no place in matters of faith? If not, why has God given us the power of reason?'

"It is reason's province to consider carefully the foundations of our faith, but its limitations must not be imposed upon by the operations of faith. And this is so because faith connects man with the power of God and brings that power into operation in his experience. Since God's power is infinite, it cannot be compassed by reason. For wherever we touch the infinite we have touched the unfathomable. Therefore the operation of faith often seems unreasonable to the one who has no faith, who ignores the infinity of God.

"The foundation of all faith is the Word of God, for faith comes by hearing, and hearing by the Word of God. Anything that does not have the Word of God as its foundation is not true faith.

"God cannot use a man more advantageously to accomplish His infinite purposes until that man comes to the place where his faith is great enough to commit him wholly to God's program, whether he understands it all or not. Let us anticipate a little, and examine a case that will illustrate this point, namely, that of Gideon, referred to in verse 32.

"The children of Israel were being greatly oppressed by the Midianites, who had overrun the land and deprived Israel of all possible means of escape, as viewed from a human standpoint. God told

Gideon that He would deliver Israel, and that He would do so by the hand of Gideon. He could not see that he was the man for that work, since he was of no special repute in the nation of Israel, and he belonged to an obscure family. Finally, he asked God for a sign. So at his request God gave him a sign one morning of a fleece full of water, but with dry ground around it. This was exactly the sign which he had asked, but he still felt distrustful. He then asked God to reverse that sign, and the next morning the ground was wet while the fleece was perfectly dry. Notice that from this point onward to complete victory nearly every step that God asked Gideon to take was an unintelligible one to him.

"Gideon called on Israel for an army. Thirty-two thousand responded, but God told him he had too many men. Twenty-two thousand of his men went home. Of the ten thousand who remained God said they were still too many. Under the Word of God the ten thousand were brought to the brook, and the men who threw themselves down in a careless manner to drink were placed in one company, while the men who had their minds on the battle and kept their eyes toward the enemy and lapped up the water while they watched, showing that their hearts were on the one enterprise, were placed in another company. Now Gideon's army was divided into two bands, one of nine thousand seven hundred, and one of three hundred. Then God said, 'By the three hundred that lapped will I save you.'

"God then told Gideon to equip his band of three hundred by giving them each an earthen vessel with a light inside; then to divide his three hundred into three bands, and surround the camp of Midian in the night, approaching it from three sides; and to break the pitchers and let the light shine forth as they shouted, 'The sword of the Lord and of Gideon' (Judges 7:18). Unsanctified reason would sneer at this, but faith moves forward at the Word of God and obtains the victory.

"God is seeking a Gideon's band today. Each one of them must have a single purpose of heart—to do their part in the final conflict with evil. Each one of us is an earthen vessel. Have we the light inside, and is the earthen vessel broken so that the light can shine? If so, we belong to Gideon's band today" (*Review and Herald*, June 12, 1924. Article by R. S. Owen).

## The Faith of the Last Church

A very impressive dream is told in *Christian Experience and Teachings of Ellen G. White*, 179–184:

There was a company of people journeying to a better country. They started with wagons heavily loaded with earthly possessions in which they trusted more or less. After going some distance the road became so steep and narrow there was not room for wagons, and they removed the most precious portion of their luggage (that in which they trusted most), and placed it on the backs of the horses and proceeded on horseback. As they progressed the path continued to narrow, and they had to press close against the wall to keep from falling over the precipice. The luggage pressed against the wall and swayed them and the horses until they were in danger of being pushed off by it. Thereupon they cut the luggage from the horses and let it fall over the precipice, and they continued on horseback. At places the path was so narrow they were still in danger of losing their balance and falling below to ruin. At such places a hand seemed to take the bridles and guide them over the difficult way. The path continued to narrow until the horses could no longer travel it and they were left behind and a few articles were carried in the hands as they continued going up the path on foot, single file. The danger of falling increased. At this point a small cord was let down from above for each person to grasp and steady himself and prevent his falling. Soon they could carry no luggage, and the last earthly possession in which they had trusted was discarded, and the cord from above grew larger and would sustain some of their weight. Now the path is so narrow that it is safer going without shoes, and they are left behind. Next, the stockings were abandoned to get the surest possible foothold. They pressed close against the wall and clung fast to the cords which were now large enough to sustain their entire weight. Then they cried to each other, 'We have hold from above! We have hold from above!' At length the path ended at a wide chasm; their entire reliance must be on the cords which had now increased in size until they were as large as their bodies. They wondered, To what are the cords attached? On the other side of the chasm was a beautiful field of green grass on which there fell a soft light like silver and gold. They hesitated in great perplexity. Presently they said, The cord is our only hope; it has helped us all the way; it will not fail us now. Someone asked, Who holds the cord? The answer was heard, 'God holds the cord; do not fear.' Then, one by one, they held to the cord and swung over the abyss into the lovely field and were safe and happy.

What was the cord which was let down from above? It was faith in God which became so strong it would wholly sustain them without trusting in any earthly thing. Such is to be the faith of the people who complete the journey in the midst of the trials, troubles and hardships of the last days. May the reader be one who has it.

# — FIVE —
# The Study of the Word of God
## *The Third Essential*

### The Place it Fills in Christian Experience

This is the third round in the ladder of an ascending Christian experience. The study of the Word of God operates in three ways for our salvation:

1. It is the guide to a correct belief.

2. It is the basis of all faith.

3. It is the vehicle of His power.

The key text for this section is Psalm 119:11. "Thy word have I hid in mine heart that I might not sin against thee."

"The reason that many professed Christians do not have a clear, well-defined experience, is that they do not think it is their privilege to understand what God has spoken through His Word" (*Fundamentals of Christian Education,* 189).

The above three ways in which the study of the Word operates will be considered separately.

### Guide to a Correct Belief

1. The Word contains the revelation of God as Creator and Redeemer, and all His plans and thoughts in which we are involved, the thoughts of God about everything that concerns us. It reveals His ideals to which we are to conform. It imparts His definition of sin, all sin, and our sin in particular; it makes the distinction and draws the line between all that is right and all that is wrong. God's only problem with men is sin—their own sin. The minister's problem, so far as the people are concerned, is to get them to see their own sins in the light of God's Word.

The Word is the standard by which all individuals and all their ideas are to be measured, and when there is a conflict between our ideas and the Word, our ideas and opinions are to be surrendered. We must always approach the study of the Word with new surrender, searching for new light that will conflict with our ideas, to which we are ready to surrender. This is the only way we can be changed. If we do not come in this spirit, He cannot teach us.

We are to study the Word not merely to learn facts, but for instruction concerning our own experience. After revealing our sins, the Word explains the penalty of sin—the consequences of sinning; and who can know these consequences and not repent of his sins? Thus the Word inspires repentance. However, there are still other ways in which it brings repentance as we shall see later. After repentance, the Word reveals the remedy-pardon, for it reveals Jesus and His tender love for the sinner and that He is waiting to give pardon, and then power to obey. Who could know that Jesus is waiting to forgive and not be sorry for his sins? Then, along with the knowledge of forgiveness the Word unfolds the wondrous price which love paid to provide the pardon, the life of the spotless Lamb of God was required to provide pardon for the smallest sin. How awful! Who could understand that and not be led to deep, sincere repentance? In all these things the Word is showing us our duty to God and to man as summarized in the *Law of God*. The same Word reveals the perfect Pattern who lived as a Man among men to show us a translation of the law of God into human conduct that we might behold its appearance and also the possibility of rendering such obedience.

For all these reasons the Word should be studied daily to keep our vision clear and to make it yet more clear. From the Word we receive wisdom, guidance, and instruction for every duty and experience, courage for the battle, cheer in discouragement, and comfort in sorrow. From it we get love for the right, love for God and man; love for the lost, for the lowest sinner and even for our enemies. From it we learn how to work for souls. From it we get hope for the future, for our eternal reward is pictured there.

## Source of Faith

2. The Word is the source of faith and the basis of faith—faith comes from its reading and also reveals that upon which our faith rests. "Faith that enables us to receive God's gifts is itself a gift, of which some measure is imparted to every human being. It grows as exercised in appropriating the Word of God. In order to strengthen faith, we must often bring it in contact with the Word" (*Education*, 253–254).

The more we study the Word, the more faith we will have, and the stronger our faith will be. None need want, for it is given here in plenitude.

## The Word of God is the Vehicle of His Power

3. Every would-be Christian is weak, and this weakness is the source of many failures because people do not understand how to lay hold of the divine power which is offered. It is contained in the Words of God. That this is true, and how that power is to operate in human lives, is now to be made very plain.

"The words that I speak unto you, they are spirit, and they are life" (John 6:63; See also John 6:48, 50, 53–58).

"The Word of God—the truth—is the channel through which the Lord manifests His Spirit and power" (*The Acts of the Apostles,* 520).

## The Power of the Word

In one of His parables, Jesus made this matter very simple to understand (see Matthew 13:16–23; Luke 8:11). Each grain of wheat had power within itself to reproduce its own kind up to one hundred. Such multiplication of grain is the act of God and is wholly beyond the power of man to do. After relating the parable, He said, "The seed is the word of God" (Luke 8:11), which is sown in the minds of men, which Word contains the same miraculous power of multiplication, so that if a person receives into his mind one of God's thoughts and holds it there as the ground holds the seed, it will *produce more thoughts of God* in the mind, it will start a *train of thoughts,* all of which will be divine like the first one received. If men and women, boys and girls, would receive only good thoughts into their minds, in due time their minds would be filled with divine thoughts, and the evil would be overcome by the power of God which is in His Word.

The multiplication of divine thoughts is as much a miracle beyond the power of man to perform as the multiplication of seed sown in the soil, and Jesus would have us learn the lesson of the power contained in God's Word from the power we know is in the seed. This is the divine ministry the Word of God is given to perform in human hearts. However, our difficulty is that we too often sow evil with the good; we feast our eyes on evil and then think about it; many people, old and young, read literature which is false, depicts the unreal, is nonsensical trash, which is like using wood, hay, and stubble to construct a building which we hope will last forever. Many people listen to unprofitable things on the radio, to gossip, and in many ways fill their minds with thoughts which will lead downward.

It should be clearly understood that *thoughts* are the *seeds* out of which grow words and *acts* which make up the life; and that the life, acts, and words cannot be renovated while evil thoughts are continually received through the wrong use of the five senses. We think about that which we see, hear, touch, taste and smell. These senses are the sources of thought. Whatever enters the mind through these gateways will later come *out* in words and deeds. The only way to control that which will come out is to control that which goes *in*.

The use we make of our five senses determines the character and destiny; this use determines what use, if any, will be made of the Word of God which is the vehicle of His power. "In order that your thoughts may be what you would have them, you must carefully select your mental food" (*Character, by* Henry Varnum, 44). "The mind, the soul, is built up by that upon which it feeds; and it rests with us to determine upon what it shall be fed. It is within the power of everyone to choose the topics that shall occupy the thoughts and shape the character" (*Education,* 126, 127). "The thoughts will be of the same character as the food we provide the mind" (*Testimonies,* vol. 5, 544). "Fill the whole heart with the Words of God. They are the living water, quenching your burning thirst. They are the Living Bread from Heaven. Jesus declares, 'Except ye eat the flesh of the Son of man, and drink his blood, ye have no life in you' (John 6:53). And He explains Himself by saying, 'The words that I speak unto you, they are spirit, and they are life' (John 6:63). Our bodies are built up from what we eat and drink; and as in the natural economy, so in the spiritual economy: it is what we meditate upon that will give tone and strength to our spiritual nature" (*Steps to Christ,* 88).

## Become Like Him Whom We Adore
"We should dwell upon the character of our dear Redeemer and Intercessor. We should meditate upon the mission of Him who came to save His people from their sins. As we thus contemplate heavenly themes, our faith and love will grow stronger, and our prayers will be more and more acceptable to God, because they will be more and more mixed with faith and love. They will be intelligent and fervent. There will be more constant confidence in Jesus, and a daily, living experience in His power to save to the uttermost all that come unto God by Him.

"As we meditate upon the perfections of the Saviour, we shall desire to be wholly transformed and renewed in the image of His purity. There will be a hungering and thirsting of soul to become like Him whom we adore. The more our thoughts are upon Christ, the more we shall speak of Him to others, and represent Him to the world" (*Ibid.,* 89).

## Guard the Avenues into the Soul
"Those who would not fall a prey to Satan's devices must guard

38

well the avenues of the soul; they must avoid reading, seeing, or hearing that which will suggest impure thoughts. The mind must not be left to dwell at random upon every subject that the adversary of souls may suggest. 'Gird up the loins of your mind' says the apostle Peter, 'be sober, and hope to the end for the grace that is to be brought unto you at the revelation of Jesus Christ; … not fashioning yourselves according to the former lusts in your ignorance: but as he which hath called you is holy, so be ye holy in all manner of conversation; because it is written, 'Be ye holy; for I am holy' [1 Peter 13–16]" (*Patriarchs and Prophets*, 460).

## Angels Weigh Our Thoughts

"I have seen an angel standing with scales in his hands weighing the thoughts and interest of the people of God, especially the young. In one scale were the thoughts and interest tending Heavenward; in the other were the thoughts and interest tending to earth. And in this scale were thrown all the reading of storybooks, thoughts of dress and show, vanity, pride, etc. Oh, what a solemn moment! the angels of God standing with scales, weighing the thoughts of His professed children—those who claim to be dead to the world and alive to God. The scale filled with thoughts of earth, vanity, and pride quickly went down, notwithstanding weight after weight rolled from the scale. The one with the thoughts and interest tending to Heaven went quickly up as the other went down, and oh, how light it was! I can relate this as I saw it; but never can I give the solemn and vivid impression stamped upon my mind, as I saw the angel with the scales weighing the thoughts and interest of the people of God. Said the angel: 'Can such enter Heaven? No, no, never. Tell them the hope they now possess is vain, and unless they speedily repent, and obtain salvation, they must perish' " (*Testimonies,* vol. 1, 124).

However there is more: when we are born our minds are biased toward evil, we have evil natures which must be *changed*. The change is not made all at once, but is a gradual process which is effected by daily receiving the thoughts of God and accepting His ideals in place of ours.

## How the Nature is Changed
## The Word Destroys the Earthly Nature

"As faith thus receives and assimilates the principles of truth, they become a part of the being and the motive power of the life. The Word of God, received into the soul, molds the thoughts, and enters into the development of character. … As they feed upon His Word, they find that it is spirit and life. The Word destroys the natural, earthly nature, and imparts a new life in Christ Jesus. The Holy Spirit comes to the soul as a Comforter. By the transforming agency of His grace, the image of God is reproduced in the disciple; he becomes a new creature. Love takes the place of hatred, and the heart receives the divine similitude. This is what it means to live 'by every word that proceedeth out of the mouth of God.' Matthew 4:4. This is eating the Bread that comes down from heaven" (*The Desire of Ages,* 391).

## When The Soul Surrenders

"When the Spirit of God takes possession of the heart, it transforms the life. Sinful thoughts are put away, evil deeds are renounced; love, humility, and peace take the place of anger, envy and strife. Joy takes the place of sadness, and the countenance reflects the light of Heaven. No one sees the hand that lifts the burden, or beholds the light that descends from the courts above. The blessing comes when by faith the soul surrenders itself to God. Then that power which no human eye can see creates a new being in the image of God" (*Ibid.,* 173).

## Purify Every Thought

"Just to the degree in which the Word of God is received and obeyed will it impress with its potency and touch with its life every spring of action, every phase of character. It will purify every thought, regulate every desire. Those who make God's Word their trust will quit themselves like men and be strong. They will rise above all baser things into an atmosphere free from defilement" (*The Ministry of Healing,* 136).

## The Reception of Christ the Word

"The reception of the Word, the Bread from Heaven, is declared to be the reception of Christ Himself. As the Word of God is received into the soul, we partake of the flesh and blood of the Son of God. As it enlightens the mind, the heart is opened still more to receive the engrafted Word, that we may grow thereby. Man is called upon to eat and masticate the Word; but unless his heart is open to the entrance of that Word, unless he drinks in the Word, unless he is taught of God, there will be a misconception, misapplication, and misinterpretation of that Word.

"As the blood is formed in the body by the food eaten, so Christ is formed within by the eating of the Word of God, which is His flesh and blood. He who feeds upon that Word has Christ formed within, the hope of glory. The Written Word introduces to the searcher

40

the flesh and blood of the Son of God; and through obedience to that Word, he becomes a partaker of the divine nature. As the necessity for temporal food cannot be supplied by once partaking of it, so the Word of God must be daily eaten to supply the spiritual necessities.

"As the life of the body is found in the blood, so spiritual life is maintained through faith in the blood of Christ. He is our life, just as in the body our life is in the blood. He is made unto us wisdom, and righteousness, and sanctification, and redemption, just as the bone, sinew, and muscle are nourished, and the whole man built up, by the circulation of the blood through the system. In vital connection with Christ, in personal contact with Him, is found health for the soul. It is the efficacy of the blood of Christ that supplies its every need and keeps it in healthy condition.

"By reason of the waste and loss, the body must be renewed with blood, by being supplied with daily food. So there is need of constantly feeding on the Word, the knowledge of which is eternal life. That Word must be our meat and drink. It is in this alone that the soul will find its nourishment and vitality. We must feast upon its precious instruction, that we may be renewed in the spirit of our mind, and grow up into Christ, our Living Head. When His Word is abiding in the living soul, there is oneness with Christ; there is a living communion with Him; there is in the soul an abiding love that is a sure evidence of our unlimited privilege.

"A soul without Christ is like a body without blood; it is dead. It may have the appearance of spiritual life; it may perform certain ceremonies in religious matters like a machine; but it has no spiritual life. So the hearing of the Word of God is not enough. Unless we are taught of God, we shall not accept the truth to the saving of our souls. It must be brought into the life practice.

"When a soul receives Christ, he receives His righteousness. He lives the life of Christ. As he trains himself to behold Christ, to study His life and practice His virtues, he eats the flesh and drinks the blood of the Son of God. When this experience is his, he can declare, with the apostle Paul: 'I am crucified with Christ: nevertheless I live; yet not I, but Christ liveth in me: and the life which I now live in the flesh I live by the faith of the Son of God, who loved me, and gave himself for me' [Galatians 2:2]" (*Review and Herald*, November 23, 1897).

## The Exalted Word of God
The Bible is the Word of the Infinite God to men; by reading it

with reverence and prayer we enter His presence and commune with Him. It is designed to minister complete redemption to those who daily live in its atmosphere—it brings the atmosphere of Heaven to sinful human beings. Yet, it is the most neglected book in the world.

A few of the most choice statements in the English language concerning the Bible are presented here with the hope that their careful, prayerful perusal will prove to be a blessing to the reader.

## The Voice of the Eternal

"With the Word of God in his hands, every human being, wherever his lot in life may be cast, may have such companionship as he shall choose. In its pages he may hold converse with the noblest and best of the human race, and may listen to the voice of the Eternal as He speaks with men. As he studies and meditates upon the themes into which 'the angels desire to look' (1 Peter 1:12), he may have their companionship. He may follow the steps of the heavenly Teacher, and listen to His Words as when He taught on mountain and plain and sea. He may dwell in this world in the atmosphere of heaven, imparting to earth's sorrowing and tempted ones thoughts of hope and longings for holiness; himself coming closer and still closer into fellowship with the Unseen; like him of old who walked with God, drawing nearer and nearer the threshold of the eternal world, until the portals shall open, and he shall enter there. He will find himself no stranger. The voices that will greet him are the voices of the holy ones, who, unseen, were on earth his companions voices that here he learned to distinguish and to love. He who through the Word of God has lived in fellowship with Heaven, will find himself at home in heaven's companionship" (*Education*, 127).

## The Bible the Supreme Educator

"No other study will so ennoble every thought, feeling, and aspiration as the study of the Scriptures. This Sacred Word is the will of God revealed to men. Here we may learn what God expects of the beings formed in His image. Here we learn how to improve the present life and how to secure the future life. No other book can satisfy the questionings of the mind and the craving of the heart. By obtaining a knowledge of God's Word, and giving heed thereto, men may rise from the lowest depths of ignorance and degradation to become the sons of God, the associates of sinless angels.

"A clear conception of what God is, and what He requires us to be, will give us humble views of self. He who studies aright the Sacred Word, will learn that human intellect is not omnipotent; that, without the help which none but God can give, human strength and wisdom are but weakness and ignorance.

"As an educating power the Bible is without a rival. Nothing will so impart vigor to all the faculties as requiring students to grasp the stupendous truths of revelation. The mind gradually adapts itself to the subjects upon which it is allowed to dwell. If occupied with commonplace matters only, to the exclusion of grand and lofty themes, it will become dwarfed and enfeebled. If never required to grapple with difficult problems, or put to the stretch to comprehend important truths, it will, after a time, almost lose the power of growth.

"The Bible is the most comprehensive and the most instructive history which men possess. It came fresh from the fountain of eternal truth, and a divine hand has preserved its purity through all the ages. Its bright rays shine into the far distant past, where human research seeks vainly to penetrate. In God's Word alone we find an authentic account of Creation. Here we behold the power that laid the foundation of the earth and that stretched out the heavens. Here only can we find a history of our race, unsullied by human prejudice or human pride.

"In the Word of God, the mind finds subject for the deepest thought, the loftiest aspiration. Here we may hold communion with patriarchs and prophets, and listen to the voice of the Eternal as He speaks with men. Here we behold the Majesty of Heaven as He humbled Himself to become our Substitute and Surety to cope with the powers of darkness and to gain the victory in our behalf. A reverent contemplation of such themes as these cannot fail to soften, purify, and ennoble the heart, and, at the same time, to inspire the mind with new strength and vigor" (*Testimonies, vol.* 5, 24, 25).

## Superior To All Other Literature

"The Bible contains all the principles that men need to understand in order to be fitted either for this life or for the life to come. And these principles may be understood by all. No one with a spirit to appreciate its teaching can read a single passage from the Bible without gaining from it some helpful thought. But the most valuable teaching of the Bible is not to be gained by occasional or disconnected study. Its great system of truth is not so presented as to be discerned by the hasty or careless reader. Many of its treasures lie far beneath the surface, and can be obtained only by diligent research and continuous effort. The truths that go to make up the great whole must be searched out and gathered up, 'here a little, and there a little' (Isaiah 28:10).

"When thus searched out and brought together, they will be found to be perfectly fitted to one another. Each Gospel is a supplement to the others, every prophecy an explanation of another, every truth a development of some other truth. The types of the Jewish economy are made plain by the Gospel. Every principle in the Word of God has its place, every fact its bearing. And the complete structure, in design and execution, bears testimony to its Author. Such a structure no mind but that of the Infinite could conceive or fashion" (*Education*, 123, 124).

## Uplifts the Highest, Reaches the Lowliest

"The Bible unfolds truths with a simplicity and a perfect adaptation to the needs and longings of the human heart, that has astonished and charmed the most highly cultivated minds, while it enables the humble and uncultured to discern the way of salvation. And yet these simply stated truths lay hold upon subjects so elevated, so far—reaching, so infinitely beyond the power of human comprehension, that we can accept them only because God has declared them. Thus the plan of redemption is laid open to us so that every soul may see the steps he is to take in repentance toward God and faith toward our Lord Jesus Christ, in order to be saved in God's appointed way; yet beneath these truths, so easily understood, lie mysteries which are the hiding of His glory—mysteries which overpower the mind in its research, yet inspire the sincere seeker for truth with reverence and faith. The more he searches the Bible, the deeper is his conviction that it is the Word of the living God, and human reason bows before the majesty of divine revelation" (*Testimonies*, vol. 5, 700).

## The Book of Books Points All to Heaven

"As an educating power, it is of more value than the writings of all the philosophers of all ages. In its wide range of style and subjects there is something to interest and instruct every mind, to ennoble every interest. The light of revelation shines undimmed into the distant past where human annals cast not a ray of light. There is poetry which has called forth the wonder and admiration of the world. In glowing beauty, in sublime and solemn majesty, in touching pathos, it is unequaled by the most brilliant productions of human genius. There is sound logic and impassioned eloquence. There are portrayed the noble deeds of noble men, examples of private virtue and public honor, lessons of piety and purity.

"There is no position in life, no phase of human experience, for which the Bible does not contain valuable instruction. Ruler and subject, master and servant, buyer and seller, borrower and lender, teacher and student—all may here find lessons of priceless worth.

"But above all else, the Word of God sets forth the plan of salvation: shows how sinful man may be reconciled to God, lays down the great principles of truth and duty which should govern our lives, and promises us divine aid in their observance. It reaches beyond this fleeting life, beyond the brief and troubled history of our race. It opens to our view the long vista of eternal ages—ages undarkened by sin, undimmed by sorrow. It teaches us how we may share the habitations of the blessed, and bids us anchor our hopes and fix our affections there" (*Review and Herald,* August 22, 1912).

We search the world for truth; we cull
The good, the pure, the beautiful,
From graven stone and written scroll,
From all old flower fields of the soul;
And, weary seekers of the best,
We come back laden from our quest,
To find that all the sages said
Is in the Book our mothers read.
—John Greenleaf Whittier

# — SIX —
## The Gospel of Health
### *The Fourth Essential*

The fourth round in the ladder of Christian experience is the gospel of health. The key text for this section is 2 Corinthians 7:1: "Having therefore these promises, dearly beloved, let us cleanse ourselves from all filthiness of the flesh and spirit, perfecting holiness in the fear of God."

There is an intimate relation between the physical and spiritual life. This scripture sets forth that thought. It is further emphasized in the following passages:

"What? Know ye not that your body is the temple of the Holy Ghost which is in you, which ye have of God, and ye are not your own? For ye are bought with a price: therefore glorify God in your body, and in your spirit, which are God's" (1 Corinthians 6:19, 20).

"Know ye not that ye are the temple of God, and that the Spirit of God dwelleth in you? If any man defile the temple of God, him shall God destroy; for the temple of God is holy, which temple ye are" (1 Corinthians 3:16, 17).

In 2 Peter 1:5, 6, temperance precedes patience. God has given all things that pertain to godliness and the divine nature (see 2 Peter 1:3, 4).

According to these scriptures the gospel must contain principles to cleanse the physical body of its defilement and facilitate the development of patience and other Christian virtues, and God will punish him who rejects and ignores these principles.

Because the fall of man occurred through the indulgence of appetite, his restoration cannot be accomplished without his conquest of appetite. This point has been made very plain in chapter four. The thought is now to be further developed.

## The Physiology of It
### Examples
### Digestion

1. The fermentation of food in the digestive tract dulls the perceptive power of the brain so that we think more slowly, do not understand as quickly as we should, and cannot comprehend

46

and use the means of redemption as we might. This makes it more difficult for us to receive guidance from God through a dull brain. This cuts down our power to perform; temptations will not be as readily discerned; and the conscience cannot be as keen.

## The Cells

2. If substances are put into the body which are injurious to the cells of the nerves, or if the elements of which these cells are made or by which they are nourished, are lacking in the nutrition so that the nerves are not being properly nourished, the nervous system becomes weakened, a long train of consequences follows, among which will be impatience, closely allied to which will be unkindness.

## Mental Powers

3. If the body is weakened, the mental powers suffer also, as mental power is the exercise of one of the organs of the body.

## Animal Passions

4. Certain types of food tend to strengthen the animal passions, such as meat and eggs, and therefore the use of such foods should be considered in connection with moral temptations and victories.

## The Power of the Will

5. The power of choice, this most precious and necessary faculty, depends upon the strength of the will. The exercise of the power of choice is disturbed when the will is weakened by the use of tea, coffee, alcohol, tobacco, opiates and narcotics, or any other will-breaking practice or habit. The power of the will is man's only means of allying himself to God. Without this he has no hope.

It is only by the exercise of the will that man can decide to submit himself to God, and a man cannot give his will to Christ while doing something which Christ forbids, which is against Christ's will, and which dominates man's will contrary to the will of Christ. The man who does not give his will to Christ is *not Christ's* (Philippians 2:13). "Both to will and to do of his good pleasure" describes the Christian.

"This will, that forms so important a factor in the character of man, was at the fall given into the control of Satan; and he has ever since been working in man to will and to do of his own good pleasure, but to the utter ruin and misery of man. But the infinite sacrifice of God in giving Jesus, His beloved Son, to become a sacrifice for sin, enables Him to say, without violating one principle of His government: 'Yield yourself up to Me; give Me that will; take it from the control of Satan, and I will take possession of it; then I can work in you to will and to do of My good pleasure.' When He gives you the mind of Christ, your will becomes as His will, and your character is transformed to be like Christ's character. Is it your purpose to do God's will? Do you wish to obey the Scriptures? 'Whosoever will come after me, let him deny himself, and take up his cross, and follow me' [Mark 8:34]" (*Testimonies*, vol. 5, 515).

"As the will of man cooperates with the will of God, it becomes omnipotent. Whatever is to be done at His command may be accomplished in His strength. All His biddings are enablings" (*Christ's Object Lessons*, 333).

"The body is to be brought into subjection. The higher powers of the being are to rule. The passions are to be controlled by the will, which is itself to be under the control of God. The kingly power of reason, sanctified by divine grace, is to bear sway in our lives" (*The Ministry of Healing,* 130).

Therefore, it is that all indulgences which injure the nerves and weaken the will *bar the way to Christian perfection.* They also shut out the Holy Spirit which is the power of God, because God will not give spiritual power to those who knowingly and willfully work against His laws of life which He maintains within the body. God must recognize the operation of His own laws of physiology, for He it is who inflicts the penalty for their violation, and He must not violate His own laws.

The body and its laws are the handiwork of the Creator, and he who truly worships and obeys Him will include these laws in his obedience. The Sabbath is the sign that man has fully surrendered to his Maker to obey every known law, and therefore the neglect or rejection of the principles of healthful living is the rejection of the principles for which the Sabbath stands.

## How to Understand Our Obligations to God

"The body is the only medium through which the mind and the soul are developed for the upbuilding of character. Hence it is that the adversary of souls directs his temptations to the enfeebling and degrading of the physical powers. His success here means the surrender to evil of the whole being. The tendencies of our physical nature, unless under the dominion of a higher power, will surely work ruin and death" (*Ibid.*).

## Choosing the Character

The mere possession of the five senses does not constitute character, but the daily proper use of them develops character. This is the field where men's priceless endowment, the power of choice, is exercised for weal or woe. The daily decisions made by the mind concerning the use of these senses shape the character and determine the destiny. Habits are formed through their exercise, and the sort of habits formed depend upon the kind of experiences chosen by the mind for the five senses to enjoy, and therefore the use or misuse of these senses will largely determine the nature of the character being developed.

## Character Made of Physical Habits

"The importance of caring for the health should be taught as a Bible requirement. Perfect obedience to God's commands calls for conformity to the laws of the being. The science of education includes as full a knowledge of physiology as can be obtained. No one can properly understand his obligations to God unless he understands clearly his obligations to himself as God's property. He who remains in sinful ignorance of the laws of life and health, or who willfully violates these laws, sins against God" (*Counsels to Parents, Teachers, and Students,* 295).

## Necessary to the Growth of Christian Character

"The indulgence of animal appetites has degraded and enslaved many. Self-denial and a restraint upon the animal appetites are necessary to elevate and establish an improved condition of health and morals, and purify corrupted society. Every violation of principle in eating and drinking blunts the perceptive faculties, making it impossible for them to appreciate or place the right value upon eternal things. It is of the greatest importance that mankind should not be ignorant in regard to the consequences of excess. Temperance in all things is necessary to health and the development and growth of a good Christian character.

"Those who transgress the laws of God in their physical organism will not be less slow to violate the law of God spoken from Sinai. Those who will not, after the light has come to them, eat and drink from principle instead of being controlled by appetite, will not be tenacious in regard to being governed by principle in other things. The agitation of the subject of reform in eating and drinking will develop character and will unerringly bring to light those who make a 'god of their bellies.' ...

"Many seem to think they have a right to treat their own bodies as they please, but they forget that their bodies are not their own. Their Creator, who formed them, has claims upon them that they cannot rightly throw off. Every needless transgression of the laws which God has established in our being is virtually a violation of the law of God, and is as great a sin in the sight of Heaven as to break the Ten Commandments. Ignorance upon this important subject is sin; the light is now beaming upon us, and we are without excuse if we do not cherish the light and become intelligent in regard to these things, which it is our highest earthly interest to understand" (*Counsels on Health*, 38–40).

## Carelessness Here Leads to Carelessness of Other Truth

"Those who are in a position where it is possible to secure a vegetarian diet, but who choose to follow their own preferences in this matter, eating and drinking as they please, will gradually grow careless of the instruction the Lord has given regarding other phases of the present truth and will lose their perception of what is truth; they will surely reap as they have sown" (*Testimonies, vol. 9*, 156, 157).

## Meat Eaters will Separate from God's People

"There are those who ought to be awake to the danger of meat eating, who are still eating the flesh of animals, thus endangering the physical, mental, and spiritual health. Many who are now only half converted on the question of meat eating will go from God's people, to walk no more with them" (*Review and Herald*, May 27, 1902).

## Physiology First Place

"So closely is health related to our happiness, that we cannot have the latter without the former. A practical knowledge of the science of human life is necessary in order to glorify God in our bodies. It is therefore of the highest importance that among the studies selected for childhood, physiology should occupy the first place. How few know anything about the structure and functions of their own bodies and of nature's laws! Many are drifting about without knowledge, like a ship at sea without compass or anchor; and what is more, they are not interested to learn how to keep their bodies in a healthy condition and prevent disease" (*Counsels on Health*, 38).

## Sin

"Transgression of physical law is transgression of the moral law; for God is as truly the Author of physical laws as He is the Author of the moral law. His law is written with His own finger upon every nerve, every muscle, every faculty, which has been entrusted to man. And every misuse of any part of our organism is a violation of that law" (*Christ's Object Lessons*, 347, 348).

## We Become Enemies of God

"God has shown that health reform is as closely connected with the third angel's message as the hand is with the body. There is nowhere to be found so great a cause of physical and moral degeneracy as a neglect of this important subject. Those who indulge appetite and passion, and close their eyes to the light for fear they will see sinful indulgences which they are unwilling to forsake, are guilty before God. Whoever turns from the light in one instance hardens his heart to disregard the light upon other matters. Whoever violates moral obligations in the matter of eating and dressing prepares the way to violate the claims of God in regard to eternal interests. Our bodies are not our own. God has claims upon us to take care of the habitation He has given us, that we may present our bodies to Him a living sacrifice, holy and acceptable. Our bodies belong to Him who made them, and we are in duty bound to become intelligent in regard to the best means of preserving them from decay. If we enfeeble the body by self-gratification, by indulging the appetite, and by dressing in accordance with health-destroying fashions, in order to be in harmony with the world, we become enemies of God" (*Testimonies*, vol. 3, 62, 63).

## A Dull Brain

"The brain is affected by the condition of the stomach. A disordered stomach is productive of a disordered, uncertain state of mind. A diseased stomach produces a diseased condition of the brain and often makes one obstinate in maintaining erroneous opinions. The supposed wisdom of such a one is foolishness with God" (*Ibid.*, vol. 7, 257).

## Leads to Rejection of Truth

"Divine truth can make little impression upon the intellect while the customs and habits are opposed to its principles. Those who are willing to inform themselves concerning the effect of sinful indulgence upon the health, and who commence the work of reform, even if it be from selfish motives, in so doing place themselves where the

51

truth of God may find access to their hearts. And, on the other hand, those who are reached by the presentation of Scripture truth are then in a position where their consciences will be aroused upon the subject of health. They see and feel the necessity of breaking away from the tyrannizing habits and appetites which have ruled them so long. There are many who would receive the truths of God's Word, their judgment having been convinced by the clearest evidence; but the carnal desires, clamoring for gratification, control the intellect, and they reject truth as falsehood, because it comes in collision with their lustful affection" (*Ibid.*, vol. 4, 553).

## First Study Eternal Destiny

"One of the strongest temptations that man has to meet is upon the point of appetite. Between the mind and the body there is a mysterious and wonderful relation. They react upon each other. To keep the body in a healthy condition to develop its strength, that every part of the living machinery may act harmoniously, should be the first study of our life. To neglect the body is to neglect the mind. It cannot be to the glory of God for His children to have sickly bodies or dwarfed minds. To indulge the taste at the expense of health is a wicked abuse of the senses. Those who engage in any species of intemperance, either in eating or in drinking, waste their physical energies and weaken moral power. They will feel the retribution which follows the transgression of physical law" (*Ibid.*, vol. 3, 485, 486).

"Indulgence of appetite is the greatest cause of physical and mental debility, and lies at the foundation of the feebleness which is apparent everywhere" (*Ibid.*, 487).

"If we could realize that the habits we form in this life will affect our eternal interests, that our eternal destiny depends upon strictly temperate habits, we would work to the point of strict temperance in eating and drinking" (*Ibid.*, 489).

## Moral Sensibilities Stupified

"Lustful appetite makes slaves of men and women, and beclouds their intellects and stupefies their moral sensibilities to such a degree that the sacred, elevated truths of God's Word are not appreciated. The lower propensities have ruled men and women.

"In order to be fitted for translation, the people of God must know themselves. They must understand in regard to their own physical frames that they may be able with the psalmist to exclaim: 'I will praise thee; for I am fearfully and wonderfully made' (Psalm 139:14). They should ever have the appetite in subjection to the moral and intellectual organs. The body should be servant to the mind, and not the mind to the body" (*Ibid.*, vol. 1, 486, 487).

## Impossible

"It is impossible for those who indulge the appetite to attain to Christian perfection" (*Ibid.*, vol. 2, 400).

"The controlling power of appetite will prove the ruin of thousands, when, if they had conquered on this point, they would have had moral power to gain the victory over every other temptation of Satan. But those who are slaves to appetite will fail in perfecting Christian character" (*Ibid.*, vol. 3, 491, 492).

## Candidates for Translation

"Again and again I have been shown that God is trying to lead us back, step by step, to His original design—that man should subsist upon the natural products of the earth. Among those who are waiting for the coming of the Lord, meat-eating will eventually be done away; flesh will cease to form a part of their diet. We should ever keep this end in view, and endeavor to work steadily toward it. I cannot think that in the practice of flesh-eating we are in harmony with the light which God has been pleased to give us" (*Christian Temperance and Bible Hygiene*, 119).

## Unfitted to be Messengers

"No man should be set apart as a teacher of the people while his own teaching or example contradicts the testimony God has given His servants to bear in regard to diet, for this will bring confusion. His disregard of health reform unfits him to stand as the Lord's messenger" (*Testimonies*, vol. 6, 378).

## Tithe, Ministers, Health Reform

"We are not to make the use of flesh food a test of fellowship, but we should consider the influence that professed believers who use flesh foods have over others. As God's messengers, shall we not say to the people: 'Whether therefore ye eat, or drink, or whatsoever ye do, do all to the glory of God' (1 Corinthians 10:31)? Shall we not bear a decided testimony against the indulgence of perverted appetite? Will any who are ministers of the gospel, proclaiming the most solemn truth ever given to mortals, set an example in returning to the flesh-pots of Egypt? Will those who are supported by the tithe from God's storehouse permit themselves by self-indulgence to poison the life-giving current flowing through their veins? Will they disregard the light and warnings that God has given them? The health of the body is to be regarded as essential for growth in grace and the acquirement of an even temper. If the stomach is not properly cared for, the formation of an upright, moral character will be hindered. The brain and nerves are in sympathy with the stomach. Erroneous eating and drinking result in erroneous thinking and acting" (*Ibid.*, vol. 9, 159, 160).

## Can We Have Confidence?

"All are now being tested and proved. Many to whom precious light has been given desire to return to the flesh-pots of Egypt. Many who are supported by the tithe from God's storehouse are by self-indulgence poisoning the life-giving current flowing through their veins. Disregarding the light God has given during the past twenty-five or thirty years, some continue to gratify their desire for flesh-meat. ... Those who use flesh-meat disregard all the warnings that God has given concerning this question. They have no evidence that they are walking in safe paths. They have not the slightest excuse for eating the flesh of dead animals. ... Can we possibly have confidence in ministers who at tables where flesh is served join with others in eating it?" (*Pacific Union Recorder,* October 9, 1902).

## We Must Act

God has placed the gospel of health within our reach *for us to use as* one of the divine means of overcoming sin and developing a Christian character. If we neglect this means and expect God to miraculously give us character just the same, that will be trying to "climb up some other way." Such a course is not of faith, but of presumption.

If we will accept and use this means, God will bless us and we shall succeed. That is *faith in God and His plan.* To ignore it is to presume that God will save us otherwise, while we do as we please.

# —— SEVEN ——
# Christian Education
## *The Fifth Essential*

### The Preparation for Life

This is the fifth round in the ladder of successful Christian experience, for it is one of the means God has given for our use in making Christian character.

Education is to prepare us for life, and if there is to be a life that has no end, the preparation for it is much more important than the preparation for this earthly life, as that life is longer than this one. Therefore Christian education is of infinitely more importance than merely secular education. If any other kind of education is gained, it will have to be unlearned or will lead to ruin.

The two texts for this section are: "The fear of the LORD is the beginning of knowledge" (Proverbs 1:7); "My son, if thou wilt receive my words, and hide my commandments with thee; so that thou incline thine ear unto wisdom, and apply thine heart to understanding; yea, if thou criest after knowledge, and liftest up thy voice for understanding; if thou seekest her as silver, and searchest for her as for hid treasures; then shalt thou understand the fear of the LORD, and find the knowledge of God. For the Lord giveth wisdom: out of his mouth cometh knowledge and understanding. He layeth up sound wisdom for the righteous: he is a buckler to them that walk uprightly. He keepeth the paths of judgment, and preserveth the way of his saints. Then shalt thou understand righteousness, and judgment, and equity; yea, every good path. When wisdom entereth into thine heart, and knowledge is pleasant unto thy soul; discretion shall preserve thee, understanding shall keep thee" (Proverbs 2:1–11).

### Non-religious Education Leads to Ruin

"It is not beyond belief that we may sometime be able to do in our laboratories what the sun is doing in its laboratory. Then it is conceivable that science could, if given the chance, transform this world within a generation.

"But to what end? Without the moral background of religion, without the spirit of service, which is the essence of religion, our new powers will only be the means of our destruction" (From interview with Robert Andrew Millikan, Ph.D., So.D., by Samuel Crowther, printed in *Collier's The National Weekly*, and reprinted in the *Homiletic Review*, December, 1926).

## Religion Founded Education

"America knows that it must have 'more than fleets and armies to satisfy the longing of the soul.' To power must be added wisdom, and to greatness must be added morality.

"It was not education that founded religion, but it was religion that founded education. It was beside the place of worship that there grew up the school.

"This important fact cannot be ignored in our development of education. Without its spirit either civilization will fall of its own weight, and that deep, abiding wisdom which supports society will cease to exist, or we shall have a type of mind keen in intelligence, but greedy and cruel; which, armed with the power of modern science in seeking to destroy, will in the end accomplish its own destruction. Without the presence of a great directing moral force, intelligence either will not be developed, or if it be developed, it will prove self-destructive. Education which is not based on religion and character is not education.

"In education the whole being must be taken into consideration. It is not enough to train the hand, the eye, to quicken the perception of the senses, develop the quickness of the intellect, and leave out of consideration the building of character, the aspirations of the soul.

"Man is far more than intelligence. It is not only what men know, but what they are disposed to do with that which they know, that will determine the rise and fall of civilization.

"We do not need more material development, we need more spiritual development. We do not need more intellectual power, we need more moral power. We do not need more knowledge, we need more character. We do not need more government, we need more culture. We do not need more law, we need more religion. We do not need more of the things that are seen, we need more of the things that are unseen. It is on that side of life that it is desirable to put the emphasis at the present time. If that side be strengthened, then either side will take care of itself. It is that side which is the foundation of all else. If the foundation be firm, the superstructure will stand. The success or failure of liberal education, the justification of its protection and encouragement by government, and of its support by society will be measured by its ability to minister to this great cause, to perform the necessary services, to make the required redeeming sacrifice" (*Review and Herald,* March 31, 1927. Article by then President of the United States of America, Calvin Coolidge).

## Proud, Vain, Bigoted

"Without the influence of divine grace, education will prove no real advantage; the learner becomes proud, vain, and bigoted. But that education which is received under the ennobling, refining influence of the Great Teacher, will elevate man in the scale of moral value with God. It will enable him to subdue pride and passion and to walk humbly before God, as dependent upon Him for every capability, every opportunity, and every privilege" (*Testimonies*, vol. 5, 32).

## Great Minds Bewildered

"The greatest minds, if not guided by the Word of God, become bewildered in their attempts to investigate the relations of science and revelation. The Creator and His works are beyond their comprehension; and because these cannot be explained by natural laws, Bible history is pronounced unreliable" (*Ibid.*, vol. 8, 258).

## Exalt Nature's Laws Above God

"So today man cannot of himself read aright the teaching of nature. Unless guided by divine wisdom, he exalts nature and the laws of nature above nature's God. This is why mere human ideas in regard to science so often contradict the teaching of God's Word. But for those who receive the light of the life of Christ, nature is again illuminated. In the light shining from the cross, we can rightly interpret nature's teaching" (*The Ministry of Healing,* 462).

## Intelligence Can Be a Greater Harm Than Ignorance

"In this generation there are many whose eyes become dazzled by the glare of human speculations, 'science falsely so called;' they discern not the net, and walk into it as readily as if blindfolded. God designed that man's intellectual powers should be held as a gift from his Maker and should be employed in the service of truth and righteousness; but when pride and ambition are cherished, and men exalt their own theories above the Word of God, then intelligence can accomplish greater harm than ignorance" (*The Great Controversy,* 573).

## Better Not to Educate

"When education in human lines is pushed to such an extent that the love of God wanes in the heart, that prayer is neglected, and that there is a failure to cultivate the spiritual attributes, it is wholly disastrous. It would be far better to cease seeking to obtain an education, and to recover your soul from its languishing condition, than to gain the best of educations, and lose sight of eternal advantages" (*Counsels to Parents, Teachers, and Students*, 412).

## Better to be Ignorant
"Can we wonder that under such circumstances some of the youth among us do not appreciate religious advantages? Can we wonder that they drift into temptation? Can we wonder that, neglected as they have been, their energies are devoted to amusements which do them no good, that their religious aspirations are weakened and their spiritual life darkened? The mind will be of the same character as that upon which it feeds, the harvest of the same nature as the seed sown. Do not these facts sufficiently show the necessity of guarding from the earliest years the education of the youth? Would it not be better for the youth to grow up in a degree of ignorance as to what is commonly accepted as education than for them to become careless in regard to the truth of God?" (*Testimonies*, vol. 6, 194).

## Choose the Life, Then Educate for It
The purpose of education is to prepare the student for life—to make a success in life. Before he can determine the kind of education to be sought he must settle on the *kind of a life* he wants to live—the purpose of the life, whether this life or eternal life, and what sort of achievements he will count to be success. True education would not prepare us to use this fleeting life in such a way as to *lose eternal life*, but would prepare us to make the highest and best use of both.

## Education That Will Endure
"Those who would be workers together with God must strive for perfection of every organ of the body and quality of the mind. True education is the preparation of the physical, mental and moral powers for the performance of every duty; it is the training of body, mind, and soul for divine service. This is the education that will endure unto eternal life" (*Christ's Object Lessons*, 330).

## The Whole Period of Existence
"True education means more than the perusal of a certain course of study. It means more than a preparation for the life that now is. It has to do with the whole being, and with the whole period of existence possible to man. It is the harmonious development of the physical, the mental, and the spiritual powers. It prepares the student for the joy

of service in this world and for the higher joy of wider service in the world to come. …

"To restore in man the image of his Maker, to bring him back to the perfection in which he was created, to promote the development of body, mind, and soul, that the divine purpose in his creation might be realized—this was to be the work of redemption. This is the object of education, the great object of life" (*Education*, 13, 15, 16).

## To Restore the Image of God

"To many, education means a knowledge of books; but 'the fear of the Lord is the beginning of wisdom.' Psalm 111:10. The true object of education is to restore the image of God in the soul. The first and most precious knowledge is the knowledge of Christ; and wise parents will keep this fact ever before the minds of their children" (*Testimonies*, vol. 5, 322).

## Education and Redemption Are One

"In the highest sense the work of education and the work of redemption are one, for in education, as in redemption, 'other foundation can no man lay than that is laid, which is Jesus Christ' (1 Corinthians 3:11). 'For it pleased the Father that in him should all fullness dwell.' [Colossians 1:19]" (*Education*, 30). Read in this connection *Testimonies*, vol. 6, 126–131 and 193–199.

## The Most Noble Work

"If ever we are to be in earnest, it is now. The enemy is pressing in on all sides, like a flood. Only the power of God can save our children from being swept away by the tide of evil. The responsibility resting upon parents, teachers, and church members, to do their part in cooperation with God, is greater than words can express.

"To train the young to become true soldiers of the Lord Jesus Christ is the most noble work ever given to man" (*Counsels to Parents, Teachers, and Students,* 166).

## Education Should Be Christian

Manifestly we cannot turn the education of our youth over to those who do not keep God's law, to those who reject His last message, oppose His work, and who will persecute His people.

It is stated that 90 per cent of the students in public schools devote themselves to the service of self or the state, and that 90 per cent of those who go through Seventh-day Adventist schools devote themselves to the service of God.

From all of these things we can see that Christian education is a means which God has given us to use in making Christian character. To make diligent use of it is a work of *faith in God*. To fail by neglect or rejection to use it and still expect God to save our children is *presumption*. We cannot overlook these and other means God has given us to use for the salvation of our children, and then read Isaiah 49:25 and conclude that prayer will offset our presumption.

# —— EIGHT ——
## Sacrifice
### *The Sixth Essential*

This is the sixth round of our ladder. God's sacrifice is told in John 3:16. He expects us to make a sacrifice, for it is through sacrifice that we enter into a covenant relationship with Him (see Psalm 50:5). It is a fact that God has made *man* responsible for carrying on His work in the earth (see Matthew 28:18–20). This involves labor, salary, transportation, equipment, supplies—everything. The entire financial burden rests upon His church. The acceptance of the gospel involves the responsibility of giving it to the world.

This means tithes for the support of the ministry; offerings for home and foreign missions; offerings to found publishing houses, schools, colleges and sanitariums; offerings and tuitions for the support of schools. These things call for constant sacrifice.

## Why Does God So Burden Us?

Does God need our help or our money? Could He not send angels to do all this work, and could not they do it much better than we? Why, then, does He lay the burden upon us?

*Answer—because we need the experience and cannot be saved without it.*

The true purpose in sacrifice is often not understood. Too often we think that the reward for our sacrifice in this world is received in the next world, while in fact we receive our chief reward here.

"God could have reached His object in saving sinners without our aid; but in order for us to develop a character like Christ's, we must share in His work" (*The Desire of Ages,* 142).

"Many who profess His name have lost sight of the fact that Christians are to represent Christ. Unless there is practical self-sacrifice for the good of others, in the family circle, in the neighborhood, in the church, and wherever we may be, then whatever our profession, we are not Christians.

"Christ has linked His interest with that of humanity, and He asks us to become one with Him for the saving of humanity" (*Ibid.,* 504).

"The true disciple will not live to gratify beloved self, but for Christ, and for the good of His little ones. He is to sacrifice his ease, his pleasure, his comfort, his convenience, his will, and his own selfish wishes for Christ's cause, or never reign with Him on His throne" (*Testimonies,* vol. 1, 85, 86).

"Those who reject the privilege of fellowship with Christ in service, reject the only training that imparts a fitness for participation with Him in His glory" (*Education,* 264).

## The Science of Sacrifice

Sin is selfishness. We naturally desire to get possessions for ourselves. Therefore God planned that in getting a Christ-like character we must give away our possessions and so wean our hearts from them. This experience in sacrifice is a foundation stone in Christian experience. It cannot be spared. This experience in sacrifice is of infinitely more value than the money raised thereby. Like as the cross of Christ—*sacrifice*—is the central thing in Christ's experience in working out the plan of salvation *so* the crucifixion of self—*our sacrifice*—is to be the center of our experience in receiving the salvation He thus wrought. It cannot be otherwise.

## Scriptures

"Jesus said unto him, If thou wilt be perfect, go and sell that thou hast, and give to the poor, and thou shalt have treasure in heaven: and come and follow me" (Matthew 19:21).

"Then said Jesus unto his disciples, If any man will come after me, let him deny himself, and take up his cross, and follow me" (Matthew 16:24).

"So likewise, whosoever he be of you that forsaketh not all that he hath, he cannot be my disciple" (Luke 14:33).

"And again I say unto you, It is easier for a camel to go through the eye of a needle, than for a rich man to enter into the kingdom of God" (Matthew 19:24).

"For the love of money is the root of all evil: which while some coveted after, they have erred from the faith, and pierced themselves through with many sorrows" (1 Timothy 6:10).

## Other Comments

"Perfection of character cannot possibly be attained without self-sacrifice" (*Testimonies,* vol. 9, 53).

"God planned the system of beneficence in order that man might become, like his Creator, benevolent and unselfish in character, and finally be a partaker with Him of the eternal, glorious reward" (*Ibid.,* vol. 4, 473).

"The Lord designed to bring man into close relationship with Himself and into sympathy and love with his fellow men by placing upon him responsibilities in deeds that would counteract selfishness and strengthen his love for God and man. The plan of system in benevolence God designed for the good of man, who is inclined to be selfish and to close his heart to generous deeds. The Lord requires gifts to be made at stated times, being so arranged that giving will become habit and benevolence be felt to be a Christian duty. The heart, opened by one gift, is not to have time to become selfishly cold and to close before the next is bestowed. The stream is to be continually flowing, thus keeping open the channel by acts of benevolence" (*Ibid.*, vol. 3, 393, 394.)

"God gives man nine-tenths, while he claims one-tenth for sacred purposes, as He has given man six days for his own work and has reserved and set apart the seventh day to Himself. For, like the Sabbath, a tenth of the increase is sacred; God has reserved it for Himself. He will carry forward His work upon the earth with the increase of the means that He has intrusted to man.

"God required of His ancient people three yearly gatherings. 'Three times in a year shall all thy males appear before the Loan thy God in the place which he shall choose; in the feast of unleavened bread, and in the feast of weeks, and in the feast of tabernacles: and they shall not appear before the Lord empty: every man shall give as he is able, according to the blessing of the Loco thy God which he hath given thee' (Deuteronomy 16:16, 17). No less than one-third of their income was devoted to sacred and religious purposes" (*Ibid.*, 395).

By this time the reader can see that character is formed by training. However, the training is God's gift and it is experienced under God's directions, and so is not of man, but of God.

Our progress in this matter of sacrifice reveals our true progress in developing the character of Christ. This is a mirror that reveals our condition. Will you let God have His way with your possessions? Will you accept His guidance in the use or disposal of them as He sees fit? Will you sacrifice for His sake as He did for your sake?

"It is more blessed to give than to receive" (Acts 20:35)—the experience is priceless—the giver gets Christ-likeness while the receiver gets only money.

## Sacrifice Makes a Miracle of Grace Possible
God will not work a miracle of grace to make you unselfish apart from the operation of His plan, which He designs shall accomplish this work. Will you accept His plan? It is one of the rungs in the ladder to heaven. We make our covenant with God by sacrifice (see Psalm 50:5).

# —— NINE ——
# Christian Service
## *The Seventh Essential*

C hristian service is the seventh and last or completing round in the ladder of Christian experience. Christian service is any single act performed, or word spoken in the name of Christ to aid any human being to know, love, and serve Him; it is the sum total of all of the efforts put forth for the rescue of lost humanity—it is the total task of the Christian church in a sinful world.

## Angels Use Human Instruments

The philosophy of Christian service is that sinner is to help sinner, rather than angels coming to do all of the work; angels work through human beings to save men; when a person gets one ray of heavenly light, he is indebted to every other person he can reach to impart that light to him. Said Paul, "I am debtor both to the Greeks, and to the Barbarians; both to the wise, and to the unwise" (Romans 1:14). "For though I preach the gospel, I have nothing to glory of: for necessity is laid upon me; yea, woe is me, if I preach not the gospel!" (1 Corinthians 9:16). Jesus said, "As my Father hath sent me, even so send I you" (John 20:21). "I will make you fishers of men" (Matthew 4:19). "Whosoever will be great among you, let him be your minister; and whosoever will be chief among you, let him be your servant: even as the Son of man came not to be ministered unto, but to minister, and to give his life a ransom for many" (Matthew 20:26–28).

"All power is given unto me in heaven and in earth. Go ye therefore, and teach all nations, baptizing them in the name of the Father, and of the Son, and of the Holy Ghost: teaching them to observe all things whatsoever I have commanded you: and, lo, I am with you alway, even unto the end of the world" (Matthew 28:18–20). Daniel wrote, "They that turn many to righteousness [shall shine] as the stars for ever and ever" (Daniel 12:3).

There is an important, basic reason why the gospel of salvation is to be carried by man to man—why the work has been committed to the church; it is this:

The sole object of redemption is to change the character of man and restore it to the likeness of the character of his Maker. God is unselfish, kind, compassionate, merciful, loving, ever seeking to bless and help those in need; the greater their need the more earnest are His efforts to supply the need; when a world was lost, He sent His Son to go and rescue it, and in Him poured out the riches of heaven in the greatest act of benevolence of all eternity, past or future. Man as a sinner is by nature selfish, unthoughtful of others, ever seeking to get for himself and add to his own comfort and possessions, with little regard for the welfare of others.

When offering redemption to the world He says to His children in the world, Please, will you do this work for me? Will you go and save the lost just as I would do if I were there? If we say, No, I do not want to do that kind of work, and I am too busy, we reveal that we are still selfish and unkind, and not like Him. If we say, Yes, Lord, I will go and do the best I can if you will teach me how to do the work and send your Spirit and angels to guide me. This attitude reveals what progress has been made in changing your own character into His likeness. And, furthermore, the change continues and is hastened by our experience in doing the work. In short, our attitude toward mankind reveals how God-like we have become; and when we reach the place that we love and work for humanity as He does, and as Jesus did when He was here, *we then have become like Him*. It is written that in the great reckoning day He will settle our destiny individually by our attitude toward needy humanity. "Inasmuch as ye have done it unto one of the least of these. ... ye have done it unto me." "Come, ye blessed of my Father, inherit the kingdom prepared for you from the foundation of the world" (Matthew 25:40, 34).

"By this shall all men know that ye are my disciples, if ye have love one to another" (John 13:35). "If a man say, I love God, and hateth his brother, he is a liar: for he that loveth not his brother whom he hath seen, how can he love God whom he hath not seen? And this commandment have we from him, That he who loveth God love his brother also" (1 John 4:20, 21).

## The Test of Our Christianity

"Love to man is the earthward manifestation of the love of God. It was to implant this love, to make us children of one family, that the King of glory became one with us. ... When we love the world as He has loved it, then for us His mission is accomplished" (*The Desire of Ages,* 641).

## Service Aids Growth
## The Christian Grows by Receiving and Giving

It is a universal law of life that exercise aids in the process of growth.

"Wherever there is life, there is increase and growth; in God's kingdom there is a constant interchange—taking in, and giving out; receiving, and returning to the Lord His own. God works with every true believer, and the light and blessings received are given out again in the work which the believer does. Thus the capacity for receiving is increased. As one imparts of the heavenly gifts, he makes room for fresh currents of grace and truth to flow into the soul from the living fountain. Greater light, increased knowledge and blessing, are his. In this work, which devolves upon every church member, is the life and growth of the church. He whose life consists in ever receiving and never giving, soon loses the blessing. If truth does not flow forth from him to others, he loses his capacity to receive. We must impart the goods of Heaven if we desire fresh blessings" (*Testimonies,* vol. 6, 448).

## Service to Man Connects us with Christ

"Christ's followers have been redeemed for service. Our Lord teaches that the true object of life is ministry. Christ Himself was a worker, and to all His followers He gives the law of service—service to God and to their fellow-men. Here Christ has presented to the world a higher conception of life than they had ever known. By living to minister for others, man is brought into connection with Christ. The law of service becomes the connecting link which binds us to God and to our fellow-men" (*Christ's Object Lessons*, 326).

## To Develop Character

"And he who seeks to give light to others will himself be blessed. 'There shall be showers of blessing' (Ezekiel 34:26). 'He that watereth shall be watered also himself' (Proverbs 11:25). God could have reached His object in saving sinners without our aid; but in order for us to develop a character like Christ's, we must share in His work. In order to enter into His joy—the joy of seeing souls redeemed by His sacrifice we must participate in His labors for their redemption" (*The Desire of Ages*, 142).

## "No Room for You in the Kingdom"

"If you do not feel that it is an honor to be a partaker of the sufferings of Christ; if you feel no burden of soul for those who are ready to perish; if you are unwilling to sacrifice that you may save means for the work that is to be done, there will be no room for you in the kingdom of God. We need to be partakers with Christ of His sufferings and self-denial at every step. We need to have the Spirit of God resting upon us, leading us to constant self-sacrifice" (*Testimonies*, vol. 9, 103, 104).

## Opposition to God

"Christ has brought us into church capacity that He may engage and engross all our capabilities in devoted service for the salvation of souls. Anything short of this is opposition to the work" (*Ibid.*, vol. 6, 447, 448). Thus it is that God has ordained Christian service as a means of grace for the development of Christian character. Those who faithfully employ it will thereby be helped toward heaven. Those who neglect it will not find any substitute, and their loss will be eternal.

## Conversion Precedes Service
### A Misapplication

Right here, someone will say, "That is just what I have been saying. If Miss Blank were only given this office or that position—delegated to do some special work—given something to *do*, it would be an encouragement to her and would lead her to take more interest in spiritual things and become more consecrated, but without it she is discouraged."

This concept of Christian service is most dangerous because it leads to confusion which is disastrous. He who holds that view has the operation of the plan of redemption reversed. God does not offer us holy work to do as an inducement to serve Him, but we are to do it as an expression of the fact that we are serving Him.

The person to whom work is offered as an inducement to serve God will by that very thing become confused in his own experience concerning how he shall become a child of God, and when he shall begin to work for God, and this confusion concerning both will prevent his progress in both. It is illogical that any person try to impart light to others which he has not yet received, or try to lead them into an experience which he himself has not yet had. Such a course not only confuses the person involved but brings confusion into the whole church: there will be a tendency to look lightly upon the qualifications for Christian service of all kinds—layman, young people's officers, and church workers all around the circle. This attitude blocks reform of many kinds within the church; it is the curse of many churches.

This important principle has been very plainly stated in the instruction given our churches. A few examples are given here:

## Our Own Feet on the Rock

"It is our own character and experience that determine our influence upon others. In order to convince others of the power of Christ's grace, we must know its power in our own hearts and lives. The gospel we present for the saving of souls must be the gospel by which our own souls are saved. Only through a living faith in Christ as a personal Saviour is it possible to make our influence felt in a skeptical world. If we would draw sinners out of the swift-running current, our own feet must be firmly set upon the Rock, Christ Jesus" (*The Ministry of Healing*, 469, 470).

## Conversion First

"God calls for workers. Personal activity is needed. But conversion comes first; seeking for the salvation of others, next.

"Spiritual despotism is to lose its hold on souls. Each one is to awake to the necessity of having a personal holiness and a personal, living faith. Then will God's work be done. Then will reformations take place. Souls will be rescued from the grasp of selfishness, and in love, patience, and Christian forbearance, will help one another to work for those perishing out of Christ." (*Review and Herald,* September 10, 1903).

## Youth First Give Themselves to
## God … Then Help Others

"In our Sabbath schools the Christian youth should be intrusted with responsibilities, that they may develop their abilities and gain spiritual power. Let the youth first give themselves to God, and then let them in their early experience be taught to help others. This work will bring their faculties into exercise and enable them to learn how to plan and how to execute their plans for the good of their associates" (*Testimonies on Sabbath School Work*, 47, 48).

## Sabbath School Workers

"The teachers should set a right example before the youth, in spirit, in deportment, and in dress.

"There cannot be a worse thing done for your Sabbath school than to place as workers young men and women who have shown great defects in their religious experience.

"In selecting officers from time to time, be sure that personal preferences do not rule, but place in positions of trust those whom you are convinced love and fear God, and who will make God their counselor" (*Ibid.*, 42, 22, 23, 84).

## All Workers

These principles apply to all who are selected and delegated to fill places of responsibility and perform special service where they stand as authorized representatives of the church—all church and Sabbath-school officers, Bible workers, pastors, evangelists and all other workers.

## Voluntary Missionary Service Open to All

Delegated office or position is not given to all, but only to those whose experience qualifies them. However, Christian missionary service is waiting for all to do without distinction. Every person who wishes to be a blessing to humanity may do so; people all around him need help of one sort or another so that none need lack for opportunity to do Christian service. If the church does not give you sufficient of it to satisfy the longings of your heart, you can find your own. This stimulant to growth in grace is open to all.

## The Holy Spirit Guides

"All who consecrate body, soul, and spirit to God's service will be constantly receiving a new endowment of physical, mental, and spiritual power. The inexhaustible supplies of heaven are at their command. Christ gives them the breath of His own Spirit, the life of His own life. The Holy Spirit puts forth its highest energies to work in heart and mind" (*Testimonies*, vol. 6, 306).

## Angels Will Direct

"All who engage in ministry are God's helping hand. They are co-workers with the angels; rather, they are the human agencies through whom the angels accomplish their mission. Angels speak through their voices, and work by their hands. And the human workers, co-operating with heavenly agencies, have the benefit of their education and experience" (*Education*, 271).

Thus the weakest being who desires to work for God may enter into His service and be divinely guided.

## The Lesson Thus Far We Have Already Revealed How the Heart is Changed
### Recapitulation

If we faithfully use God's appointed means for our transformation

1. Prayer
2. Faith

69

3. The Study of the Word of God
4. The Gospel of Health
5. Christian Education
6. Sacrifice
7. Christian Service

*God will see that our hearts are changed.* He does the miracle while we do these seven things: His Holy Spirit is administering these seven experiences to us and directing us in their use, and as we cooperate with Him in using these plans *His Spirit changes our natures into the divine likeness.*

## Our Part is Small But Necessary

"The power of God is the one element of efficiency in the grand work of obtaining the victory over the world, the flesh, and the devil. It is in accordance with the divine plan that we follow every ray of light given of God. Man can accomplish nothing without God, and God has arranged His plans so as to accomplish nothing in the restoration of the human race without the cooperation of the human with the divine. The part man is required to sustain is immeasurably small, yet in the plan of God it is just that force that is needed to make the work a success" (*Manuscript Releases,* vol. 10, 306).

"We are laborers together with God. This is the Lord's own wise arrangement. The cooperation of the human will and endeavor with divine energy is the link that binds men up with one another and with God. The apostle says, 'We are labourers together with God: ye are God's husbandry, ye are God's building' (1 Corinthians 3:9). Man is to work with the faculties God has given him. 'Work out your own salvation with fear and trembling.' He says; 'for it is God that worketh in you both to will and to do of his good pleasure' [Philippians 2:12, 13]" (*Mind, Character, and Personality,* vol. 2, 694).

## A Complete Christian Experience

Will the reader please note that this presentation of the gospel of health places it as one factor in seven, all of which are necessary to comprise a complete Christian experience; that it keeps the health factor in proper relation to the other six, and does not minimize or encroach upon any of the other basic phases of the experience. The seven being thus well-balanced, it cannot be said that health reform in this setting is unbalanced.

# ── TEN ──
# Living by the Spirit

## The Spirit Works Through the Seven Essentials

There is much confusion concerning the Holy Spirit, what it is to do for Christians, how it may be received in a larger measure, how its work is related to the seven "rounds of the ladder" presented in the preceding chapters, the meaning and place of the "fruits of the Spirit" and the "gifts of the Spirit," the place of miracles and healings in the church, and many other phases of the work of the Spirit. The present chapter undertakes to clear away this confusion.

Text, Galatians 5:25: "If we live in the Spirit, let us also walk in the Spirit." This text introduces a thought which is kept ever before the Christian in the Bible—the place and work of the Holy Spirit in Christian experience.

This treatise is dealing with the problems of Christian experience in character building and gaining the victory over sin, and has presented *seven means* which God has given us *to use* to assist in this task, prayer, faith, study of the Word, the gospel of health, Christian education, sacrifice, and Christian service. The question now to be studied is this: What relation does the *Holy Spirit* sustain *to man 's use of these seven means?* Are they in opposition to each other? Are they two separate and distinct ways or methods of attacking the problem of the victorious life?

Let it be understood now that these means are not in opposition to the Holy Spirit, and they are not a substitute for its work; neither can the work of the Holy Spirit be made a substitute for them; but rather the Holy Spirit *uses these means and operates through them.*

That this relationship of cooperation may be made very clear, each one of these essentials will now be discussed again with this point especially in view.

## 1. Prayer and the Holy Spirit

### Spirit Teaches Us to Pray

"Likewise the Spirit also helpeth our infirmities: for we know

71

not what we should pray for as we ought: but the Spirit itself maketh intercession for us with groanings which cannot be uttered. And he that searcheth the hearts knoweth what is the mind of the Spirit, because he maketh intercession for the saints according to the will of God" (Romans 8:26, 27).

## Prayer is Inspired by the Spirit

"We must not only pray in Christ's name, but by the inspiration of the Holy Spirit" (*Christ's Object Lessons,* 147).

"But ye, beloved, building up yourselves on your most holy faith, praying in the Holy Ghost, keep yourselves in the love of God, looking for the mercy of our Lord Jesus Christ unto eternal life" (Jude 20, 21).

Therefore it is that *prayer* and the *Holy Spirit* do not operate separately for our spiritual growth, but unitedly, for the Spirit is teaching us how to pray and inditing the prayer. If we seek to separate the two we will destroy the work of both.

## Surrender

Furthermore, the attitude in prayer must be that of definite surrender of everything in the life to the Spirit, which is summed up in the phrase, *"Thy will be done."* It is useless for us to pray in any other way. The Holy Spirit and the principle of surrender govern the prayer, and the degree of surrender determines how much we are blessed through prayer.

Prayer cannot be substituted for the Spirit, nor the Spirit for prayer. Prayer, surrender, and the Spirit are a divine trio working together for our transformation. This may sound too simple to occupy our time in this study, but the meaning is mighty and will be more apparent as we proceed.

## Get More of the Spirit

The Spirit is the still small voice ever leading us to more prayer. If, when it speaks to us and calls us to prayer, we listen and step aside for communion with God as it suggests, the Spirit comes into our hearts in greater plentitude. But, if we say we have not time, or give some other reason, or defer the matter until some later time, the Spirit is rebuffed and withdraws from us to the extent that we fail to heed its admonition. This is one way we lose the Spirit from our lives.

Moreover, to yield to the Spirit's call to prayer is one item in the total experience of surrender to Him. We do not surrender to God all at one bound, but item by item as we pass through life's daily experience.

We do come to a place where we make a great surrender, but after that, there may be occurrences every hour of the day which call for a new or more complete surrender.

## 2. Faith and the Holy Spirit

"God hath dealt to every man the measure of faith" (Romans 12:3). This measure of faith is given through the Spirit. "To another faith by the same Spirit" (1 Corinthians 12:9).

Therefore *faith* and the *Spirit* do not operate *separately* for our development, but unitedly. The Spirit is imparting the faith and urging us to believe God. If we seek to separate them we destroy the work of both.

### Surrender

The attitude we sustain to faith must be that of definite surrender of everything in the life contrary to *faith in Christ.* It is useless to try to exercise faith apart from each surrender. *Faith accepts God,* which is but surrender stated in another way. The degree of surrender reveals the extent of our faith.

Faith cannot be substituted for the Spirit, nor the Spirit for faith. Faith, surrender, and the Spirit form another trio working together for our salvation.

### More of the Spirit

The Spirit is always trying to get us to believe in God and in His Word, while it is natural for us to doubt. When it says, Be not faithless but believing, if I say, "Very well, Lord, I accept the lesson," the Spirit comes into the heart in a larger measure. However, if I reply, "I cannot accept the lesson, it is too hard, I cannot understand it, I cannot see where it will lead me," then the Spirit remains away, and I suffer the loss.

## 3. The Study of the Word and the Holy Spirit

### The Spirit Teaches The Word

"But the Comforter, which is the Holy Ghost, whom the Father will send in my name, he shall teach you all things, and bring all things to your remembrance, whatsoever I have said unto you" (John 14:26).

"Howbeit when he, the Spirit of truth is come, he will guide you into all truth: for he shall not speak of himself; but whatsoever he shall hear, that shall he speak: and he will show you things to come" (John 16:13).

"But ye have an unction from the Holy One, and ye know all things." 'But the anointing which ye have received of him abideth in you, and ye need not that any man teach you: but as the same anointing teacheth you of all things, and is truth, and is no lie, and even as it hath taught you, ye shall abide in him" (1 John 2:20, 27).

"But God hath revealed them unto us by his Spirit: for the Spirit searcheth all things, yea, the deep things of God" (1 Corinthians 2:10).

The Spirit teacheth us all we ever learn from the Word of God. Therefore our study of the Word and the work of the Spirit operate together to restore the likeness of God in the soul.

If we try to separate the two we *destroy the work of both.*

## Surrender

Our approach to the study of the Bible and the Testimonies must always be with a readiness to yield to the will of God as soon as it is discovered. It is useless to try to study them in any other spirit. Surrender to what we have learned and our readiness to yield to what we shall learn determine, to a large extent, how much the Spirit will reveal to us now.

The study of the Word cannot be substituted for the work of the Spirit, nor the work of the Spirit for it. Study of the Word, surrender to it, and the work of the Spirit, form still another divine trio working together for our salvation.

## More of the Spirit

The Spirit is ever calling us to more faithful study of the Word of God, and to a more complete acceptance of it. If we neglect its admonition to study, or to own and read other writings which God has provided for our salvation, the Spirit turns away and waits for us to heed the call, and we have less of its presence than we might have.

## 4. The Gospel of Health and the Holy Spirit

"Know ye not that ye are the temple of God, and that the Spirit of God dwelleth in you? If any man defile the temple of God, him shall God destroy; for the temple of God is holy, which temple ye are" (1 Corinthians 3:16, 17).

"What? know ye not that your body is the temple of the Holy Ghost which is in you, which ye have of God, and ye are not your own? For ye are bought with a price: therefore glorify God in your body, and in your spirit, which are God's" (1 Corinthians 6:19, 20.)

"Having therefore these promises, dearly beloved, let us cleanse ourselves from all filthiness of the flesh and spirit, perfecting holiness in the fear of God" (2 Corinthians 7:1).

These scriptures make it clear that the gospel of health and the Spirit are *fellow workers—that* they do not work separately upon us, but *unitedly.*

This cleansing of the body includes healthful living.

"The health reform, I was shown, is a part of the third angel's message and is just as closely connected with it as are the arm and hand with the human body. I saw that we as a people must make an advance move in this great work. Ministers and people must act in concert. God's people are not prepared for the loud cry of the third angel. They have a work to do for themselves which they should not leave for God to do for them. He has left this work for them to do. It is an individual work; one cannot do it for another. 'Having therefore these promises, dearly beloved, let us cleanse ourselves from all filthiness of the flesh and spirit, perfecting holiness in the fear of God' (2 Corinthians 7:1). Gluttony is the prevailing sin of this age. Lustful appetite makes slaves of men and women, and beclouds their intellects and stupefies their moral sensibilities to such a degree that the sacred, elevated truths of God's Word are not appreciated. The lower propensities have ruled men and women" (*Testimonies, vol. 1,* 486).

*The Holy Spirit demands a clean temple to dwell in.* The Spirit teaches us out of the Bible and the Testimonies what right living is and guides us in the application and use of its principles.

## Surrender

To the extent we surrender to the Spirit's teaching of those principles, He will give us the victory over evil habits and desires, and make us fit dwelling places for Himself.

If we try to separate the gospel of health from the work of the Holy Spirit we destroy the power of both. Such separation removes the health message from the realm of the spiritual and lowers it to the level of the physical, making it to be only a matter of physiology. In this way its binding claims are released and its spiritual benefits lost, and it is removed from its divine setting in the last presentation of the Gospel.

## More of the Spirit

The degree to which the Spirit can have its way with us in the matter of healthful living and health habits has much to do with the measure of the Spirit which abides with us. Millions of people have driven the Spirit from their lives by gross indulgence. Thousands more have grieved Him by lesser indulgences. He comes into our hearts or stays out according to our treatment of His pleading voice. The decision and the consequences are ours.

# 5. Christian Education and the Holy Spirit

Education comes to men through the Spirit.

"For to one is given by the Spirit the word of wisdom; to another the word of knowledge by the same Spirit" (1 Corinthians 12:8).

The relation between Christian education and the Spirit has always been definite and clear. So far as this movement is concerned, the principles of Christian education came through the Spirit of Prophecy. In ancient times the schools were under the direct supervision of the prophets so that education was directed by the Spirit of God.

Therefore the principles of Christian education and the Holy Spirit do not operate separately for our advancement, but unitedly. The Spirit gives us the principles and directs in their use.

If we separate education from the Spirit we destroy the power of both.

## Surrender

The amount of blessing we receive from education depends largely upon how fully we surrender to the guidance of the Spirit in giving, obtaining, and using it.

Even Christian education cannot be made a substitute for the work of the Spirit nor the work of the Spirit for education. They, with surrender, form another trio to work for our salvation.

## More of the Spirit

In this phase of Christian experience we can increase or lessen the measure of the Spirit within by our attitude toward its counsel.

# 6. Sacrifice and the Holy Spirit

Under the administration of the Spirit, the believers in Jerusalem in the times of persecution had all things common (see Acts 4:31–35). This one scripture is sufficient to show that the Spirit produces the spirit of sacrifice within us.

Therefore the experience in sacrifice and the work of the Spirit are not operating separately for our spiritual growth, but unitedly. The Spirit would direct in the sacrifice and in the use of the funds, and operate upon the giver's heart to make him Christ-like by the acts of sacrifice.

If we separate sacrifice from the work of the Spirit and make it mechanical merely, we will destroy the blessing of both.

## Surrender

The amount of blessing we receive in Christlikeness of character through sacrifice depends upon how fully we surrender to the Spirit of Christ in sacrifice and enter into His experience in sacrifice from His standpoint.

Sacrifice, therefore, cannot be made a substitute for the work of the Spirit, nor the work of the Spirit for it.

The Holy Spirit uses it as a means to make us Christ-like. He performs the miracle within us when we yield and decide to perform the acts of sacrifice.

## More of The Spirit

If we hear His voice calling to greater liberality, He comes within in larger measure. If we decline, He remains away.

## 7. Christian Service and the Holy Spirit

The Holy Spirit directs in all matters of service (see Acts 8:26–40; Acts 16:6–10).

Christian service and the Spirit do not work separately for us but unitedly. If we would separate them we would destroy the holy work of both.

## Surrender

The degree to which the spirit will guide any person in work for others, and the amount of blessing in Christlikeness of character which we receive from the experiences of Christian service depend upon how fully we surrender to the Spirit of Christ in rendering the service.

Christian service cannot be made a substitute for the work of the Spirit, nor the work of the Spirit for it; but they, with the surrender, form another trio which work to develop a Christ-like character within us.

## More of the Spirit

Christ is yearning over every sinner on earth, and He sends His Spirit to all who have light, to hasten with it to those who have it not. The neglect to heed this call is one of the greatest sins of Christendom. And, if there be a last church knowing from the prophecies that the end of all things is near, beyond which there will be no more opportunity to be saved, a supreme duty would be to herald that message to every susceptible soul in the world. To neglect to do so would largely shut the Spirit out, while to heed His call to that task will bring the Spirit in sufficient power to make it possible to do the work and to do it well. The decision is ours.

## How Much of the Spirit Do You Want?

Each person has working in his heart and life *as much of the Spirit as he desires.* This may startle some reader, but if you will now review the foregoing pages beginning with the subtitle *"Living by the Spirit"* you can see that it is even so.

The Holy Spirit is about each person, like the atmospheric pressure, trying to find a way in. He will come in and take possession just to the extent you yield to His voice and receive His counsel. You make the decision, and you take the consequence.

## Related Scriptures

A few scriptures which discuss the work of the Holy Spirit will now be studied that the reader may understand that throughout the Bible the work of grace carried on by the Spirit is *not done independently of these seven means of grace* we have been discussing, but that the Spirit works through these channels, and that when we read the scripture promises of the work of the Spirit upon our individual hearts to make us Christ-like we should so understand them.

- John 3:1–8. The experience of the new birth does not come through the Spirit apart from prayer, faith, Bible study, and so forth, but in connection with them.

- Philippians 2:13. God does not work "to will and to do" in us by His Spirit *apart* from these seven means, but rather *through* them.

- Galatians 2:20. "Christ liveth in me" by His Spirit working in connection with all these delegated agencies we have been studying.

- Romans 8:4. We walk "after the Spirit" as He pilots us in the reception and use of the means of grace God has appointed.

- Galatians 5:22–24. The Holy Spirit will bear His fruits in our individual lives if we yield fully to Him, and follow His leading in the use of every means of grace God has given.

- Galatians 5:25, 26. We will "live in the Spirit" when every act, thought, and plan of life is shaped by the Spirit as He indites our prayers, inspires our faith, teaches us the Word, guides us in following the laws of health, directs in education, has His way in sacrifice, and leads in Christian service.

These principles are beautifully summarized in 2 Peter 1:1–11, where it is said that God has thus given unto us "all things that pertain unto life and godliness;" and that by these means we "might be partakers of the divine nature;" that "if ye do these things, ye shall never fall;" and that if we "give diligence" to these things we shall make our "calling and election sure," "for so an entrance shall be ministered unto you abundantly into the everlasting kingdom of our Lord and Saviour Jesus Christ." Thus has God wondrously provided for the complete restoration of His likeness in man.

## Receiving The Spirit

If the Christian is asked, "Have you received the Spirit?" he will surely say, "Yes, I could not live the Christian life without the constant companionship and aid of the Holy Spirit." However, this would not mean that he had received the "gifts" of the Spirit like tongues, or healings, or prophecy, which God sometimes bestows to give power for witnessing. He means that he has surrendered to the Spirit to direct his life in molding his character in bearing the "fruits" of the Spirit.

## The "Fruits" and "Gifts" of The Spirit

These two terms are names of two different functions of the Holy Spirit, and the relation between the two is seldom understood because even most Christian people do not clearly distinguish one from the other; it might be true of the one now reading these lines.

The "fruits" of the Spirit are "love, joy, peace, long-suffering, gentleness, goodness, faith, meekness, temperance" (Galatians 5:22). They are brought forth by the Spirit as He works upon the heart of the individual through the seven means already discussed, calling for repentance, obedience and then re-creating the nature. This work goes on *within the heart,* without outward show or demonstration except a godly life, and is for the salvation of the person in whom they are developed. *This experience is positively necessary to his salvation. There is no other way.*

The purpose and function of the "gifts" of the Spirit are quite different; they are not given for the benefit of the one receiving them, but are given to increase his power and efficiency in working for other people. The "gifts" are given only to holy men who have already had a deep experience in bearing the "fruits" of the Spirit.

## The Miraculous in the Experience

Every change in making the heart purer is a miraculous act of the Holy Spirit. The conception of Christian experience as set forth in this treatise does not eliminate or seek to subdue the miraculous working of the Holy Spirit upon the heart and in the life, but does seek to show its place and what we are to do to make it possible. Remember, He works through the seven means we have been studying.

"The life-giving power of the Holy Spirit, proceeding from the Saviour, pervades the soul, renews the motives and affections, and brings even the thoughts into obedience to the will of God, enabling the receiver to bear the precious fruit of holy deeds" (*The Acts of the Apostles*, 284).

## Laws That Govern

The Spirit's work within a person, to produce the "fruits" and make him holy, is done as he surrenders to and cooperates with the Spirit, but it is done according to the laws God has established governing spiritual things and spiritual growth. "There are great laws that govern the world of nature, and spiritual things are controlled by principles equally certain. The means for an end must be employed, if the desired results are attained" (*Testimonies*, vol. 9, 221). Christian growth occurs according to law.

## The Greater Miraculous

The Holy Spirit in His work often goes beyond working through established laws and does something extra as in a miracle of healing, or the giving of special wisdom as He did for Daniel and his companions, but this greater miraculous is done when we are in harmony with and co-operating with the operations of the Spirit in administering the seven means discussed in these lessons, and *not* when we are *opposed* to or neglecting them.

# — ELEVEN —
## Seeking the Spirit

Every passage in the Bible and the Testimonies concerning the Holy Spirit presents it as the great essential to success in the Christian experience, and over and over again we are urged to seek and pray for it. When we do so, for *what sort of manifestation of it should we seek?*

Answer: Usually not for its phenomena, but rather that it should operate through or in connection with prayer, faith, the study *of* the Word, healthful living, education, sacrifice and service *for the development of a perfect character.*

When we ask God to give us more of His Spirit, *He wants to know our attitude toward each of these seven avenues through which His Spirit is to work for us.* If we are against any of them, or neglect them, we are against the Spirit and against God, and the added measure of His Spirit cannot be forthcoming until we change our attitude.

Seeking for *these experiences* in the Spirit is not seeking for the "gifts"—that is *another matter* which must not be confused with these. That comes later, as God wills (see 1 Corinthians 12:11).

To seek for the phenomena or outward demonstrations of the Spirit in place of these seven experiences administered by the Spirit is to bring *confusion* into the experience and into the church, because it is to seek for an outward demonstration ahead of the development of character, and to put "gifts" ahead of the "fruits," which is out of God's order. The members of the remnant church who are doing that are falling into Satan's trap set especially for them to deceive the very elect. Satan's most subtle deceptions for those who know the prophecies and understand that the second coming of Christ is near, is not concerning any of the great doctrines of the Bible about which there is so much disagreement in the churches of today. He knows they are grounded in doctrine, and he does not try so hard to disturb them in that realm; but while they are confidently enjoying their doctrines, he confuses them concerning their own Christian experience.

To seek for the "gifts" ahead of the "fruits" is one of the fundamental errors of those who make much of "getting the Spirit"; it is seeking for a demonstration of the phenomena of the Spirit without due regard to seeking for obedience first.

It is right to pray for the "gifts" and for the "latter rain," but only for the right purpose, not *for victory, but for witnessing! To reverse this is confusion!*

## The Gifts of the Spirit

The "gifts" are set forth in 1 Corinthians 12:1, 4–11, 28, and Ephesians 4:7, 11–15, and may be listed as follows:

| | |
|---|---|
| Apostles | Helps |
| Prophets | Governments |
| Evangelists | Knowledge |
| Pastors | Wisdom |
| Teachers | Faith |
| Miracles | Discernment of Spirits |
| Healings | Interpretation of tongues |
| Diversities of tongues | Prophecy, etc., etc. |

These "gifts" are to operate, as God wills, through those who have already had a deep experience in the "fruits," and cause them to work for those who have not yet borne the "fruits." The "gifts" operate through holy men to give power to their witnessing to develop holy character in others.

## Only Holy Men Have Gifts

2 Peter 1:21—"holy men"

Luke 2:25–26—"just and devout."

Acts 8:14–24—Those whose "hearts" are "right."

The "upper chamber" came before Pentecost.

When praying to God for more of His Holy Spirit, we should always remember that His first mission is to "reprove the world of sin" (John 16:8), to show us that we are sinners, not to bestow the gift of tongues or of healings.

## Victory Over Sin is to Come First; "Gifts" of the Spirit, and the Outpouring of the Latter Rain Come Later

This matter has been made very plain in the guiding literature of the last church. Some of the instruction is reproduced here:

"I was shown that if God's people make no efforts on their part, but wait for the refreshing to come upon them and remove their wrongs and correct their errors; if they depend upon that to cleanse them from filthiness of the flesh and spirit, and fit them to engage in the loud cry of the third angel, they will be found wanting. The refreshing or power of God comes only on those who have prepared themselves for it by doing the work which God bids them, namely, cleansing themselves from all filthiness of the flesh and spirit, perfecting holiness in the fear of God" (*Testimonies*, vol. 1, 619).

"Those who come up to every point, and stand every test, and overcome, be the price what it may, have heeded the counsel of the True Witness, and they will receive the latter rain, and thus be fitted for translation" (*Ibid.*, 187).

"Not one of us will ever receive the seal of God while our characters have one spot or stain upon them. It is left with us to remedy the defects in our characters, to cleanse the soul temple of every defilement. Then the latter rain will fall upon us as the early rain fell upon the disciples on the Day of Pentecost" (*Ibid.*, vol. 5, 214).

"The Spirit can never be poured out while variance and bitterness toward one another are cherished by the members of the church. Envy, jealousy, evil surmising, and evil speaking are of Satan, and they effectually bar the way against the Holy Spirit's working" (*Ibid.*, vol. 6, 42).

"When we bring our hearts into unity with Christ, and our lives into harmony with His work, the Spirit that fell on the disciples on the Day of Pentecost will fall on us" (*Ibid.*, vol. 8, 246).

"I saw that none could share the 'refreshing' unless they obtain the victory over every besetment, over pride, selfishness, love of the world, and over every wrong word and action. We should, therefore, be drawing nearer and nearer to the Lord and be earnestly seeking that preparation necessary to enable us to stand in the battle in the day of the Lord. Let all remember that God is holy and that none but holy beings can ever dwell in His presence" (*Early Writings*, 71).

"The health reform, I was shown, is a part of the third angel's message and is just as closely connected with it as are the arm and hand with the human body. I saw that we as a people must make an advance move in this great work. Ministers and people must act in concert. God's people are not prepared for the loud cry of the third angel. They have a work to do for themselves which they should not leave for God to do for them. He has left this work for them to do. It is an individual work; one cannot do it for another. 'Having therefore these promises, dearly beloved, let us cleanse ourselves from all filthiness of the flesh and spirit, perfecting holiness in the fear of God' (2 Corinthians 7:10). Gluttony is the prevailing sin of this age. Lustful appetite makes slaves of men and women, and beclouds their intellects and stupefies their moral sensibilities to such a degree that the sacred, elevated truths of

God's Word are not appreciated. The lower propensities have ruled men and women" (*Testimonies*, vol. 1, 486).

"The warfare against God's law, which was begun in heaven, will be continued until the end of time. Every man will be tested. Obedience or disobedience is the question to be decided by the whole world. All will be called to choose between the law of God and the laws of men. Here the dividing line will be drawn. There will be but two classes. Every character will be fully developed; and all will show whether they have chosen the side of loyalty or that of rebellion. Then the end will come" (*The Desire of Ages*, 763).

"Christ is waiting with longing desire for the manifestation of Himself in His church. When the character of Christ shall be perfectly reproduced in His people, then He will come to claim them as His own" (*Christ's Object Lessons*, 69).

# TWELVE

# The Purpose of the Gifts at Pentecost

## Surrender First

T he gifts of Pentecost were not given for the advancement of the apostles in their own Christian experience or to give them the victory over sin, as they did not receive the outpouring "until through faith and prayer the disciples had surrendered themselves fully for His working" (*Ibid.*, 327).

## Not for Themselves

"Before the day of Pentecost they met together, and put away all differences. They were of one accord. They believed Christ's promise that the blessing would be given, and they prayed in faith. They did not ask for a blessing for themselves merely; they were weighted with the burden for the salvation of souls. The gospel was to be carried to the uttermost parts of the earth, and they claimed the endowment of power that Christ had promised. Then it was that the Holy Spirit was poured out, and thousands were converted in a day.

"So it may be now, instead of man's speculations, let the Word of God be preached. Let Christians put away their dissensions, and give themselves to God for the saving of the lost. Let them in faith ask for the blessing, and it will come. The outpouring of the Spirit in apostolic days was the 'former rain,' and glorious was the result. But the latter rain will be more abundant" (*Review and Herald,* November 19, 1908).

## Peter Not Changed by Pentecost, But Before

"When the crowing of the cock reminded him of the Words of Christ, surprised and shocked at what he had just done he turned and looked at his Master. At that moment Christ looked at Peter, and beneath that grieved look, in which compassion and love for him were blended, Peter understood himself. He went out and wept bitterly. That look of Christ's broke his heart. Peter had come to the turning point, and bitterly did he repent his sin. He was like the publican in his contrition and repentance, and like the publican he found mercy. The look of Christ assured him of pardon.

"Now his self-confidence was gone. Never again were the old boastful assertions repeated.

"Christ after His resurrection thrice tested Peter. 'Simon, son of Jonas,' He said, 'lovest thou me more than these?' Peter did not now exalt himself above his brethren. He appealed to the One who could read his heart. 'Lord,' he said, 'thou knowest all things; thou knowest that I love thee' (John 21:15, 17). "Then he received his commission" (*Christ's Object Lessons,* 152–154).

"Peter was naturally forward and impulsive, and Satan had taken advantage of these characteristics to overthrow him. Just before the fall of Peter, Jesus had said to him, 'Satan hath desired to have you, that he may sift you as wheat: but I have prayed for thee, that thy faith fail not: and when thou art converted, strengthen thy brethren' (Luke 22:31, 32). That time had now come, and the transformation in Peter was evident. The close, testing questions of the Lord had not called out one forward, self-sufficient reply; and because of his humiliation and repentance, Peter was better prepared than ever before to act as shepherd to the flock. ...

"Before his fall, Peter was always speaking unadvisedly, from the impulse of the moment. He was always ready to correct others, and to express his mind, before he had a clear comprehension of himself or of what he had to say. But the converted Peter was very different. He retained his former fervor, but the grace of Christ regulated his zeal. He was no longer impetuous, self-confident, and self-exalted, but calm, self-possessed, and teachable. He could then feed the lambs as well as the sheep of Christ's flock" (*The Desire of Ages,* 812–815).

Those who reverse the purpose of the gifts of the Spirit at Pentecost and teach that it was Pentecost which made the change in Peter's spiritual condition, will also reverse the purpose of the "latter rain" and teach the church to *look to it as a means of victory* over sin when that time shall come and so teach men to pray for the manifestation of the "gifts" when they should be praying for the "fruits." This brings *confusion* into their experience and into the church and hinders the progress of the individuals, and defers the finishing of God's work in the earth when they think they are doing the opposite. Those who hold that view of Pentecost and of the "latter rain" are confused in their own experience and are confusing God's people.

# — THIRTEEN —
# Cautions

## Not to Wait for the Latter Rain to Do for Us That Which the Spirit Must Do as "Fruits" Before That Time

### Many Will Be Lost

"I saw that many were neglecting the preparation so needful, and were looking to the time of 'refreshing' and the 'latter rain' to fit them to stand in the day of the Lord and to live in His sight. Oh, how many I saw in the time of trouble without a shelter! They had neglected the needful preparation; therefore they could not receive the refreshing that all must have to fit them to live in the sight of a holy God. Those who refuse to be hewed by the prophets and fail to purify their souls in obeying the whole truth, and who are willing to believe that their condition is far better than it really is, will come up to the time of the falling of the plagues, and then see that they needed to be hewed and squared for the building. But there will be no time then to do it and no Mediator to plead their cause before the Father. Before this time the awfully solemn declaration has gone forth, 'He that is unjust, let him be unjust still: and he which is filthy, let him be filthy still: and he that is righteous, let him be righteous still: and he that is holy, let him be holy still' (Revelation 22:11).

"I saw that none could share the 'refreshing' unless they obtain the victory over every besetment, over pride, selfishness, love of the world, and every wrong word and action. We should, therefore, be drawing nearer and nearer to the Lord and be earnestly seeking the preparation necessary to enable us to stand in the battle in the day of the Lord. Let all remember that God is holy and that none but holy beings can ever dwell in His presence" (*Early Writings*, 71).

### Those Who Fail to Receive Former Rain Will Not Receive Latter

"'Ask ye of the Lord rain in the time of the latter rain; so the Lord shall make bright clouds, and give them showers of rain'

(Zechariah 10:1). 'He will cause to come down for you the rain, the former rain, and the latter rain' (Joel 2:23). In the East the former rain falls at the sowing time. It is necessary in order that the seed may germinate. Under the influence of the fertilizing showers, the tender shoot springs up. The latter rain, falling near the close of the season, ripens the grain and prepares it for the sickle. The Lord employs these operations of nature to represent the work of the Holy Spirit. As the dew and the rain are given first to cause the seed to germinate, and then to ripen the harvest, so the Holy Spirit is given to carry forward, from one stage to another, the process of spiritual growth. The ripening of the grain represents the completion of the work of God's grace in the soul. By the power of the Holy Spirit the moral image of God is to be perfected in the character. We are to be wholly transformed into the likeness of Christ.

"The latter rain, ripening earth's harvest, represents the spiritual grace that prepares the church for the coming of the Son of man. But unless the former rain has fallen, there will be no life; the green blade will not spring up. Unless the early showers have done their work, the latter rain can bring no seed to perfection.

"There is to be 'first the blade, then the ear, after that the full corn in the ear' (Mark 4:28). There must be a constant development of Christian virtue, a constant advancement in Christian experience. This we should seek with intensity of desire, that we may adorn the doctrine of Christ our Saviour.

"Many have in a great measure failed to receive the former rain. They have not obtained all the benefits that God has thus provided for them. They expect that the lack will be supplied by the latter rain. When the richest abundance of grace shall be bestowed, they intend to open their hearts to receive it. They are making a terrible mistake. The work that God has begun in the human heart in giving His light and knowledge must be continually going forward. Every individual must realize his own necessity. The heart must be emptied of every defilement and cleansed for the indwelling of the Spirit. It was by the confession and forsaking of sin, by earnest prayer and consecration of themselves to God, that the early disciples prepared for the outpouring of the Holy Spirit on the Day of Pentecost. The same work, only in greater degree, must be done now. Then the human agent had only to ask for the blessing, and wait for the Lord to perfect the work concerning him. It is God who began the work, and He will finish His work, making man complete in Jesus Christ. But there must be no neglect of the grace represented by the former rain. Only those who are living up to the light they have will receive greater light. Unless we are daily advancing in the exemplification of the active Christian virtues, we shall not recognize the manifestations of the Holy Spirit in the latter rain. It may be falling on hearts all around us, but we shall not discern or receive it" (*Testimonies to Ministers,* 506, 507).

"We may be sure that when the Holy Spirit is poured out those who did not receive and appreciate the early rain will not see or understand the value of the latter rain" (*Ibid.,* 399).

"There is to be in the churches a wonderful manifestation of the power of God, but it will not move upon those who have not humbled themselves before the Lord, and opened the door of their hearts by confession and repentance. In the manifestation of that power which lightens the earth with the glory of God, they will see only something which in their blindness they think dangerous, something which will arouse their fears, and they will brace themselves to resist it. Because the Lord does not work according to their expectations and ideas, they will oppose the work. 'Why,' they say, 'should we not know the Spirit of God when we have been in the work so many years?' … Because they did not respond to the warnings, the entreaties, of the messages of God, but persistently said, 'I am rich and increased with goods, and have need of nothing.' "

"Talent, long experience, will not make men channels of light unless they place themselves under the bright beams of the Sun of righteousness, and are called and chosen, and prepared by the endowment of the Holy Spirit" (*Review and Herald,* December 23, 1890).

## Men May Not Recognize Loud Cry
## God Will Use Simple Means

"Unless those who can help in _____ are aroused to a sense of their duty, they will not recognize the work of God when the loud cry of the third angel shall be heard. When light goes forth to lighten the earth, instead of coming up to the help of the Lord, they will want to bind about His work to meet their narrow ideas. Let me tell you that the Lord will work in this last work in a manner very much out of the common order of things, and in a way that will be contrary to any human planning. There will be those among us who will always want to control the work of God, to dictate even what movements shall be made when the work goes forward under the direction of the angel who joins the third angel in the message to be given to the world. God will use ways and means by which it will be seen that He is taking the reins in His own hands. The workers will be surprised by the simple means that He will use to bring about and perfect His work of righteousness" (*Testimonies to Ministers,* 300).

These statements make it plain that there are *two kinds* of experiences given through the Holy Spirit—one for *our* salvation and the other to operate *through* us for *others;* that the first is called the "former rain" or the "fruits," and the other the "latter rain" or the "gifts," and that to seek for the work of the Spirit in any other manner is futile and fatal.

# ——— FOURTEEN ———
## The Shaking of the Remnant Church by Heresy, Apostasy, and Persecution

A s set forth in section eleven, the latter rain in its fullness is not poured out upon sinners. The church is being and is to be "shaken," and much of the dross taken out and the chaff separated from the wheat by the three agencies named in this heading.

Many people will be shaken out of the last church, but there will be those who "cannot be shaken" and will "remain." The elect will be those who "remain"—the unshakable ones (see Hebrews 12:25–29).

"Satan has come down with great power to work with all deceivableness of unrighteousness in them that perish; and everything that can be shaken will be shaken, and those things that cannot be shaken will remain. The Lord is coming very soon, and we are entering into scenes of calamity" (*Testimonies*, vol. 9, 62).

Satan fights the remnant church most fiercely (see Revelation 12:17).

Peter was "sifted as wheat." We shall be likewise sifted (Luke 22:31).

Satan's last masterful temptation in the church will be to seek to deceive the elect at the last moment (see Matthew 24:24).

All nations are to be "shaken" (see Haggai 2:6, 7).

Many members of the seventh and last church of time will be "spued out" of the mouth of Jehovah because they are satisfied with their condition, refuse to open their eyes to see themselves as He sees them, and correct the deficiencies in their Christian experience; their knowledge of prophecies and doctrines cannot save them (see Revelation 3:14–22).

Among those who are looking for the coming of the Lord are many (perhaps half of the church members) who will not prepare their hearts to meet Him; they are careless; they expect to get ready, but when He comes they will still be unready and though they beg to be admitted, the door is "shut," and the Voice from within replies, "I know you not" (Matthew 25:1–13).

## Truth Can Either Save or Ruin

"Great blessings and privileges are ours. We may secure the most valuable heavenly treasures. Let ministers and people remember that gospel truth ruins if it does not save. The soul that refuses to listen to the invitations of mercy from day to day can soon listen to the most urgent appeals without an emotion stirring the soul" (*Testimonies*, vol. 5, 134).

To listen to truth but refuse to heed and follow it, hardens the heart, and it will meet us in the judgment. This is the way truth "ruins if it does not save." It is unsafe to delay to heed the voice of God when He speaks and gives us light.

## Shaking From Within

The last church will be shaken by influences operating within the church: "I asked the meaning of the shaking I had seen and was shown that it would be caused by the straight testimony called forth by the counsel of the True Witness to the Laodiceans. This will have its effect upon the heart of the receiver, and will lead him to exalt the standard and pour forth the straight truth. Some will not bear this straight testimony. They will rise up against it, and this is what will cause a shaking among God's people" (*Early Writings*, 270; read pages 269–273, and also *Testimonies*, vol. 1, 179–184).

In other words, there will be those who teach and follow the "straight testimony," and others who will not, and the agitation and conflict resulting will shake and divide the church. The bone of contention will be the standards fixed by the "straight testimony."

The present and future conditions in the remnant church were faithfully and minutely portrayed many years ago in *Testimonies*, vol. 5, 76, 84, 207–216.

In those pages are revealed conflicting influences operating within the church, one toward the world and the other toward holiness; widespread unbelief in the *Testimonies;* "supreme homage" given to "science falsely so called"; the light of many "stars" going out; "few great men" engaged in the closing work because "they are self-sufficient, independent of God, and He cannot use them"; men finishing the work who were "taught rather by the unction of His Spirit, than by the outward training of scientific institutions"; popular apostasy; shaking and sifting which separate the false from the true and thus purify the church; the sealing of the true ones; the coming of the power of the latter rain; the last gospel message completed, and the final victory of the church. These pages reveal that many of the same conflicts which are raging between the church and the world are being repeated within the church. The enemy presses his battle over eternal principles into every quarter, including the remnant church. Note carefully the following sections of this book:

## Shaken by Heresy

"Until Christ shall appear in the clouds of heaven with power and great glory, men will become perverse in spirit and turn from the truth to fables. The church will yet see troubleous times. She will prophesy in sackcloth. But although she must meet heresies and persecutions, although she must battle with the infidel and the apostate, yet by the help of God she is bruising the head of Satan. The Lord will have a people as true as steel, and with faith as firm as the granite rock. They are to be His witnesses in the world, His instrumentalities to do a special, a glorious work in the day of His preparation" (*Testimonies*, vol. 4, 594, 595).

"God will arouse His people; if other means fail, heresies will come in among them, which will sift them, separating the chaff from the wheat" (*Gospel Workers*, 299).

"God's Spirit has illuminated every page of Holy Writ, but there are those upon whom it makes little impression, because it is imperfectly understood. When the shaking comes, by the introduction of false theories, these surface readers, anchored nowhere, are like shifting sand" (*Testimonies to Ministers,* 112).

## Shaken by Apostasy

Herewith are reproduced a few other outstanding statements in the *Testimonies* concerning a strong tendency toward apostasy in the remnant church:

## Small Number Saved

"From what was shown me, but a small number of those now professing to believe the truth would eventually be saved—not because they could not be saved, but because they would not be saved in God's own appointed way. The way marked out by our divine Lord is too narrow and the gate too strait to admit them while grasping the world or while cherishing selfishness or sin of any kind. There is no room for these things; and yet there are but few who will consent to part with them, that they may pass the narrow way and enter the strait gate" (*Testimonies*, vol. 2, 445, 446).

## A Small Portion Sanctified

"We are living in a most solemn time. In the last vision given me, I was shown the startling fact that but a small portion of those who now profess the truth will be sanctified by it and be saved. Many will get above the simplicity of the work. They will conform to the world, cherish idols, and become spiritually dead. The humble, self-sacrificing followers of Jesus will pass on to perfection, leaving behind the indifferent and lovers of the world" (*Ibid.*, vol. 1, 608, 609).

## Danger Greater Than Israel
"I was pointed back to ancient Israel. But two of the adults of the vast army that left Egypt entered the land of Canaan. Their dead bodies were strewn in the wilderness because of their transgressions. Modern Israel are in greater danger of forgetting God and being led into idolatry than were His ancient people. Many idols are worshiped, even by professed Sabbathkeepers. God especially charged His ancient people to guard against idolatry, for if they should be led away from serving the living God, His curse would rest upon them, while if they would love Him with all their heart, with all their soul, and with all their might, He would abundantly bless them in basket and in store, and would remove sickness from the midst of them" (*Ibid.*, 609).

## Repeating Israel's History
"Satan's snares are laid for us as verily as they were laid for the children of Israel just prior to their entrance into the land of Canaan. We are repeating the history of that people. Lightness, vanity, love of ease and pleasure, selfishness, and impurity are increasing among us. There is need now of men who are firm and fearless in declaring the whole counsel of God; men who will not sleep as do others, but watch and be sober. Knowing as I do the great lack of holiness and power with our ministers, I am deeply pained to see the efforts for self-exaltation. If they could but see Jesus as He is, and themselves as they are, so weak, so inefficient, so unlike their Master, they would say: If my name may be written in the obscurest part of the book of life, it is enough for me, so unworthy am I of His notice" (*Ibid.*, vol. 5, 160).

## Disobedience Greater Than Jewish Church
"The same disobedience and failure which were seen in the Jewish church have characterized in a greater degree the people who have had this great light from Heaven in the last message of warning. Shall we, like them, squander our opportunities and privileges until God shall permit oppression and persecution to come upon us? Will the work which might be performed in peace and comparative prosperity be left undone until it must be performed in days of darkness, under the pressure of trial and persecution?" (*Ibid.*, 456, 457).

## Following Ancient Israel

"Gather up the rays of light that have been slighted and rejected. Gather them up with meekness, with trembling, and with fear. The sin of ancient Israel was in disregarding the expressed will of God and following their own way according to the leadings of unsanctified hearts. Modem Israel are fast following in their footsteps, and the displeasure of the Lord is as surely resting upon them" (*Ibid.*, 94).

## Like Jews at First Advent

"I have seen that self-glorification was becoming common among Seventh-day Adventists and that unless the pride of man should be abased and Christ exalted we should, as a people, be in no better condition to receive Christ at His second advent than were the Jewish people to receive Him at His first advent" (*Ibid.*, 727, 728).

## Christ Pronounced a Woe

"I have been shown that the spirit of the world is fast leavening the church. You are following the same path as did ancient Israel. There is the same falling away from your holy calling as God's peculiar people. You are having fellowship with the unfruitful works of darkness. Your concord with unbelievers has provoked the Lord's displeasure. You know not the things that belong to your peace, and they are fast being hid from your eyes. Your neglect to follow the light will place you in a more unfavorable position than the Jews upon whom Christ pronounced a woe. ... There are only a few who, like stars in a tempestuous night, shine here and there among the clouds.

"Many who complacently listen to the truths from God's Word are dead spiritually, while they profess to live. For years they have come and gone in our congregations, but they seem only less and less sensible of the value of revealed truth. They do not hunger and thirst after righteousness. They have no relish for spiritual or divine things. They assent to the truth, but are not sanctified through it" (*Ibid.*, 75, 76).

## Not One in Twenty

"Not one in twenty whose names are registered upon the church books are prepared to close their earthly history, and would be as verily without God and without hope in the world as the common sinner. They are professedly serving God, but are more earnestly serving Mammon. This half-and-half work is a constant denying of Christ, rather than a confession of Christ. So many have brought into the church their own unsubdued spirit, unrefined; their spiritual taste is perverted by their own immoral, debasing, corruptions, symbolizing the world in spirit,

95

in heart, in purpose, confirming themselves in lustful practices, and are full of deception through and through in their professed Christian life. Living as sinners, claiming to be Christians. Those who claim to be Christians and will confess Christ should come out from among them and touch not the unclean thing, and be separate. ...

"I lay down my pen and lift up my soul in prayer, that the Lord would breathe upon his backsliding people, which are as dry bones, that they may live. The end is near, stealing upon us so stealthily, so imperceptibly, so noiselessly, like the muffled tread of the thief in the night to surprise the sleepers off guard and unready. May the Lord grant to bring His Holy Spirit upon hearts that are now at ease, that they may no longer sleep as do others, but watch and be sober" (*General Conference Bulletin,* February 4, 1893).

## False Prophecy and Miracles

"Many have a name to live while they have become spiritually dead. These will one day say: 'Lord, Lord, have we not prophesied in thy name? and in thy name cast out devils? and in thy name done many wonderful works? And then will I profess unto them, I never knew you: depart from me, ye that work iniquity' [Matthew 7:22, 23]" (*Testimonies,* vol. 5, 73).

## False Prophecy

"Many will stand in our pulpits with the torch of false prophecy in their hands, kindled from the hellish torch of Satan. If doubts and unbelief are cherished, the faithful ministers will be removed from the people who think they know so much. 'If thou hadst known,' said Christ, 'even thou, at least in this thy day, the things which belong unto thy peace! but now they are hid from thine eyes' [Luke 19:42]" (*Testimonies to Ministers,* 409, 410).

## Apostasy

"As Jesus views the state of His professed followers today, He sees base ingratitude, hollow formalism, hypocritical insincerity, Pharisaical pride and apostasy" (*Testimonies,* vol. 5, 72).

## Satan Unsettles Faith

"Great changes are soon to take place in the world, and everyone will need an experimental knowledge of the things of God. It is the work of Satan to dishearten the people of God and to unsettle their faith" (*Ibid.,* 273).

## Few Preserve Faith in Purity

"The earnest prayers of this faithful few will not be in vain. When the Lord comes forth as an avenger, He will also come as a protector of all those who have preserved the faith in its purity and kept themselves unspotted from the world. It is at this time that God has promised to avenge His own elect which cry day and night unto Him, though He bear long with them" (*Ibid.*, 210).

## Help Sufficient for Our Needs

God does not thus describe the conditions in His church to drive anyone to despair; He offers the remedy, but it will not be accepted and used unless we know our need; therefore He is trying to help us to understand how desperate is our need.

## Shaken by Persecution
## Persecution Reveals Condition

"Soon God's people will be tested by fiery trials, and the great proportion of those who now appear to be genuine and true will prove to be base metal" (*Ibid.*, 136).

## Many Stars Go Out

"The time is not far distant when the test will come to every soul. The mark of the beast will be urged upon us. Those who have step-by-step yielded to worldly demands and conformed to worldly customs will not find it a hard matter to yield to the powers that be, rather than subject themselves to derision, insult, threatened imprisonment, and death. The contest is between the commandments of God and the commandments of men. In this time the gold will be separated from the dross in the church. True godliness will be clearly distinguished from the appearance and tinsel of it. Many a star that we have admired for its brilliancy will then go out in darkness. Chaff like a cloud will be borne away on the wind, even from places where we see only floors of rich wheat. All who assume the ornaments of the sanctuary, but are not clothed with Christ's righteousness, will appear in the shame of their own nakedness.

"When trees without fruit are cut down as cumberers of the ground, when multitudes of false brethren are distinguished from the true, then the hidden ones will be revealed to view, and with hosannas range under the banner of Christ. Those who have been timid and self-distrustful will declare themselves openly for Christ and His truth. The most weak and hesitating in the church will be as David— willing to do and dare. The deeper the night for God's people, the

97

more brilliant the stars. Satan will sorely harass the faithful; but, in the name of Jesus, they will come off more than conquerors. Then will the church of Christ appear 'fair as the moon, clear as the sun, and terrible as an army with banners' [Song of Solomon 6:10]" (*Ibid.*, 81, 82).

## Go Out and Oppose

"As the storm approaches, a large class who have professed faith in the third angel's message, but have not been sanctified through obedience to the truth, abandon their position and join the ranks of the opposition. By uniting with the world and partaking of its spirit, they have come to view matters in nearly the same light; and when the test is brought, they are prepared to choose the easy, popular side" (*The Great Controversy,* 608).

## Will Be a Division

"As trials thicken around us, both separation and unity will be seen in our ranks. Some who are now ready to take up weapons of warfare will in times of real peril make it manifest that they have not built upon the solid rock; they will yield to temptation. Those who have had great light and precious privileges, but have not improved them, will, under one pretext or another, go out from us. Not having received the love of the truth, they will be taken in the delusions of the enemy; they will give heed to seducing spirits and doctrines of devils, and will depart from the faith. But, on the other hand, when the storm of persecution really breaks upon us, the true sheep will hear the true Shepherd's voice. Self-denying efforts will be put forth to save the lost, and many who have strayed from the fold will come back to follow the great Shepherd. The people of God will draw together and present to the enemy a united front. In view of the common peril, strife for supremacy will cease; there will be no disputing as to who shall be accounted greatest. Not one of the true believers will say: 'I am of Paul; and I of Apollos; and I of Cephas' (1 Corinthians 1: 12). The testimony of one and all will be: 'I cleave unto Christ; I rejoice in Him as my personal Saviour.'

## Clean Church Gives Loud Cry

"Thus will the truth be brought into practical life, and thus will be answered the prayer of Christ, uttered just before His humiliation and death: 'That they all may be one; as thou, Father, art in me, and I in thee, that they also may be one in us: that the world may believe that thou hast sent me' (John 17:21). The love of Christ, the love of our brethren will testify to the world that we have been with Jesus and learned of Him. Then will the message of the third angel swell to a loud cry, and the whole earth will be lightened with the glory of the Lord" (*Testimonies,* vol. 6, 400, 401).

## The Shaking Is Followed by Great Power
## A Reformation Movement

"In visions of the night, representations passed before me of a great reformatory movement among God's people. Many were praising God. The sick were healed, and other miracles were wrought. A spirit of intercession was seen, even as was manifested before the great day of Pentecost. Hundreds and thousands were seen visiting families and opening before them the Word of God. Hearts were convicted by the power of the Holy Spirit, and a spirit of genuine conversion was manifest. On every side doors were thrown open to the proclamation of the truth. The world seemed to be lightened with the heavenly influence. Great blessings were received by the true and humble people of God. I heard voices of thanksgiving and praise, and there seemed to be a reformation such as we witnessed in 1844" (*Ibid.,* vol. 9, 126).

## Great Power—Loud Cry

"The numbers of this company had lessened. Some had been shaken out and left by the way. The careless and indifferent, who did not join with those who prized victory and salvation enough to perseveringly plead and agonize for it, did not obtain it, and they were left behind in darkness, and their places were immediately filled by others taking hold of the truth and coming into the ranks. Evil angels still pressed around them, but could have no power over them.

"I heard those clothed with the armor speak forth the truth with great power. It had effect. Many had been bound; some wives by their husbands, and some children by their parents. The honest who had been prevented from hearing the truth now eagerly laid hold upon it. All fear of their relatives was gone, and the truth alone was exalted to them. They had been hungering and thirsting for truth; it was dearer and more precious than life. I asked what had made this great change. An angel answered, 'It is the latter rain, the refreshing from the presence of the Lord, the loud cry of the third angel' " (*Early Writings,* 271).

## Like Pentecost

"The work will be similar to that of the day of Pentecost. As the 'former rain' was given, in the outpouring of the Holy Spirit at the opening of the gospel, to cause the upspringing of the precious seed, so the 'latter rain' will be given at its close for the ripening of the harvest. 'Then shall we know, if we follow on to know the Lord: His going forth is prepared as the morning; and he shall come unto us as the rain, as the latter and former rain unto the earth' (Hosea 6:3). 'Be glad then, ye children of Zion, and rejoice in the LORD your God: for he hath given you the former rain moderately, and he will cause to come down for you the rain, the former rain, and the latter rain' (Joel 2:23). 'In the last days, saith God, I will pour out my Spirit upon all flesh.' 'And it shall come to pass, that whosoever shall call on the name of the Lord shall be saved' (Acts 2:17, 21).

"The great work of the gospel is not to close with less manifestation of the power of God than marked its opening. The prophecies which were fulfilled in the outpouring of the former rain at the opening of the gospel are again to be fulfilled in the latter rain at its close. Here are 'the times of refreshing' to which the apostle Peter looked forward when he said: 'Repent ye therefore, and be converted, that your sins may be blotted out, when the times of refreshing shall come from the presence of the Lord; and he shall send Jesus' (Acts 3:19, 20).

"Servants of God, with their faces lighted up and shining with holy consecration, will hasten from place to place to proclaim the message from heaven. By thousands of voices, all over the earth, the warning will be given. Miracles will be wrought, the sick will be healed, and signs and wonders will follow the believers. Satan also works, with lying wonders, even bringing down fire from heaven in the sight of men (see Revelation 13:13). Thus the inhabitants of the earth will be brought to take their stand.

"The message will be carried not so much by argument as by the deep conviction of the Spirit of God. The arguments have been presented. The seed has been sown, and now it will spring up and bear fruit. The publications distributed by missionary workers have exerted their influence, yet many whose minds were impressed have been prevented from fully comprehending the truth or from yielding obedience. Now the rays of light penetrate everywhere, the truth is seen in its clearness, and the honest children of God sever the bands which have held them. Family connections, church relations, are powerless to stay them now. Truth is more precious than all besides. Notwithstanding the agencies combined against the truth, a large number take their stand upon the Lord's side" (*The Great Controversy,* 611, 612).

## Gift of Tongues Repeated

"It is with an earnest longing that I look forward to the time when the events of the day of Pentecost shall be repeated with even greater power than on that occasion. John says, 'I saw another angel come

100

down from heaven, having great power; and the earth was lightened with his glory.' Revelation 18:1. Then, as at the Pentecostal season, the people will hear the truth spoken to them, every man in his own tongue. God can breathe the new life into every soul that sincerely desires to serve Him, and can touch the lips with a live coal from off the altar, and cause them to become eloquent with His praise. Thousands of voices will be imbued with the power to speak forth the wonderful truths of God's Word. The stammering tongue will be unloosed, and the timid will be made strong to bear courageous testimony to the truth. May the Lord help His people to cleanse the soul temple from every defilement, and to maintain such a close connection with Him that they may be partakers of the latter rain when it shall be poured out" (*Review and Herald,* July 20,1886).

## The Final Victory

"In vision I saw two armies in terrible conflict. One army was led by banners bearing the world's insignia; the other was led by the blood-stained banner of Prince Immanuel. Standard after standard was left to trail in the dust as company after company from the Lord's army joined the foe and tribe after tribe from the ranks of the enemy united with the commandment-keeping people of God. An angel flying in the midst of heaven put the standard of Immanuel into many hands, while a mighty general cried with a loud voice: 'Come into line. Let those who are loyal to the commandments of God and the testimony of Christ now take their position. Come out from among them, and be ye separate, and touch not the unclean, and I will receive you, and will be a Father unto you, and ye shall be My sons and daughters. Let all who will come up to the help of the Lord, to the help of the Lord against the mighty.'

"The battle raged. Victory alternated from side to side. Now the soldiers of the cross gave way, 'as when a standard-bearer fainteth' (Isaiah 10:18). But their apparent retreat was but to gain a more advantageous position. Shouts of joy were heard. A song of praise to God went up, and angel voices united in the song, as Christ's soldiers planted His banner on the walls of fortresses till then held by the enemy. The Captain of our salvation was ordering the battle and sending support to His soldiers. His power was mightily displayed, encouraging them to press the battle to the gates. He taught them terrible things in righteousness as He led them on step by step, conquering and to conquer.

"At last the victory was gained. The army following the banner with the inscription, 'The commandments of God, and the faith of

101

Jesus,' was gloriously triumphant. The soldiers of Christ were close beside the gates of the city, and with joy the city received her King. The kingdom of peace and joy and everlasting righteousness was established" (*Testimonies,* vol. 8, 41, 42).

## The Triumph

Thus God in His church triumphs with the power of the latter rain which comes upon purified people.

# ─── FIFTEEN ───
# The Place of Miraculous Healing in the Advent Movement

T hroughout this book an important place is given to miracles of healing in the true church; and yet, miracles are not to be a test of the true church, nor are they to be the means of carrying forward the work. In several sections of the book, warnings against Satanic miracles will be found. Before we proceed to deal further with false miracles which will be wrought to delude the people into believing it is unnecessary to observe the laws of health to get well, we wish at this point to insert, almost parenthetically, a short chapter giving clear statements from the Testimonies that miracles are in order, why we do not have more of them, and how to proceed when we pray for the recovery of the sick.

## God Will Heal Now

"God is just as willing to restore the sick to health now as when the Holy Spirit spoke these Words through the psalmist. And Christ is the same compassionate Physician now that He was during His earthly ministry. In Him there is healing balm for every disease, restoring power for every infirmity. His disciples in this time are to pray for the sick as verily as the disciples of old prayed. And recoveries will follow; for 'the prayer of faith shall save the sick.' (James 5:15). We have the Holy Spirit's power, the calm assurance of faith, that can claim God's promises. The Lord's promise, 'They shall lay hands on the sick, and they shall recover' (Mark 16:18), is just as trustworthy now as in the days of the apostles. It presents the privilege of God's children, and our faith should lay hold of all that it embraces. Christ's servants are the channel of His working, and through them He desires to exercise His healing power. It is our work to present the sick and suffering to God in the arms of our faith. We should teach them to believe in the great Healer" (*The Ministry of Healing*, 226).

## How to Pray for the Sick

"As to praying for the sick, it is too important a matter to be handled carelessly. I believe we should take everything to the Lord, and make known to God all our weaknesses, and specify all our perplexities.

When in sorrow, when uncertain as to what course to pursue, two or three who are accustomed to pray should unite together in asking the Lord to let His light shine upon them, and to impart His special grace; and He will respect their petitions, He will answer their prayers. If we are under infirmities of body it is certainly consistent to trust in the Lord, making supplications to our God in our own case, and if we feel inclined to ask others in whom we have confidence, to unite with us in prayer to Jesus who is the Mighty Healer, help will surely come if we ask in faith. I think we are altogether too faithless, too cold and lukewarm.

"I understand the text in James is to be carried out when a person is sick upon his bed; if he calls for the elders of the church, and they carry out the directions in James, anointing the sick with oil, in the name of the Lord, praying over him the prayer of faith. We read, 'The prayer of faith shall save the sick, and the Lord shall raise him up; and if he have committed sins, they shall be forgiven him' (James 5:15).

"It cannot be our duty to call for the elders of the church for every little ailment we have, for this would be putting a task upon the elders. If all should do this, their time would be fully employed, they could do nothing else; but the Lord gives us the privilege of seeking Him individually in earnest prayer, of unburdening our souls to Him, keeping nothing from Him who has invited us, 'Come unto me, all ye that labor and are heavy laden, and I will give you rest' (Matthew 11:28). Oh how grateful we should be that Jesus is willing and able to bear all our infirmities and strengthen and heal all our diseases if it will be for our good and for His glory. Some died in the days of Christ and in the days of the apostles because the Lord knew just what was best for them. I would not speak one word to lessen your faith and perplex and worry you. There is never danger of our being too much in earnest and having too much confidence and trust in God. Be of good courage; look to Jesus constantly.

## God's Doctors—Simple Remedies

"Now in regard to that which we can do for ourselves, there is a point that requires careful, thoughtful consideration. I must become acquainted with myself. I must be a learner always as to how to take care of this building, the body God has given me, that I may preserve it in the very best condition of health. I must eat those things which will be for my very best good physically, and I must take special care to have my clothing such as will conduce to a healthful circulation of the blood. I must not deprive myself of exercise and air. I must get all the sunlight that it is possible for me to obtain. I must have wisdom to be a faithful guardian of my body.

"I should do a very unwise thing to enter a cool room in a perspiration; I should show myself an unwise steward to allow myself to sit in a draft and thus expose myself so as to take cold. I should be unwise to sit with cold feet and limbs and thus drive back the blood from the extremities to the brain or internal organs. I should always protect my feet in damp weather. I should eat regularly of the most healthful food which will make the best quality of blood, and I should not work intemperately if it is in my power to avoid doing so. And when I violate the laws God has established in my being, I am to repent and reform, and place myself in the most favorable condition under the doctors God has provided—pure air, pure water, and the healing, precious sunlight.

"Water can be used in many ways to relieve suffering. Draughts of clear, hot water taken before eating (half a quart, more or less), will never do any harm, but will rather be productive of good. A cup of tea made from catnip herb will quiet the nerves. Hop tea will induce sleep. Hop poultices over the stomach will relieve pain. If the eyes are weak, if there is pain in the eyes, or inflammation, soft flannel cloths wet in hot water and salt, will bring relief quickly. When the head is congested, if the feet and limbs are put in a bath with a little mustard, relief will be obtained. There are many more simple remedies which will do much to restore healthful action to the body. All these simple preparations the Lord expects us to use for ourselves, but man's extremities are God's opportunities.

## Presumption

"If we neglect to do that which is within the reach of nearly every family, and ask the Lord to relieve pain, when we are too indolent to make use of these remedies within our power, it is simply presumption. The Lord expects us to work in order that we obtain food. He does not propose that we shall gather the harvest unless we break the sod, till the soil, and cultivate the produce. Then God sends the rain and the sunshine and the clouds to cause vegetation to flourish. God works and man cooperates with God. Then there is seedtime and harvest. God has caused to grow out of the ground, herbs for the use of man, and if we understand the nature of those roots and herbs, and make a right use of them, there would not be a necessity of running for the doctor, so frequently, and people would be in better health than they are today" (*Paulson Collection*, 28, 29).

## Cease to Transgress

"It is labor lost to teach people to look to God as a healer of their infirmities, unless they are taught also to lay aside unhealthful practices. In order to receive His blessing in answer to prayer, they must cease to do evil and learn to do well. Their surroundings must be sanitary, their habits of life correct. They must live in harmony with the law of God, both natural and spiritual" (*The Ministry of Healing,* 227, 228).

## Many Prayers are Presumptuous

"In the Word of God we have instruction relative to special prayer for the recovery of the sick. But the offering of such prayer is a most solemn act, and should not be entered upon without careful consideration. In many cases of prayer for the healing of the sick, that which is called faith is nothing less than presumption" (*Ibid.*).

## Drugs and Miracles Clash

"Those who will gratify their appetite, and then suffer because of their intemperance, and take drugs to relieve them, may be assured that God will not interpose to save health and life which is so recklessly periled. The cause has produced the effect. Many, as their last resort, follow the directions in the Word of God, and request the prayers of the elders of the church for their restoration to health. God does not see fit to answer prayers offered in behalf of such, for He knows that if they should be restored to health, they would again sacrifice it upon the altar of unhealthy appetite" (*Spiritual Gifts,* vol. 4, 145).

## God Must Not Transgress

"Should the Lord work a miracle to restore the wonderfully fine machinery which human beings through their own carelessness and inattention, and their indulgence of appetite and passions, have destroyed in doing the very things the Lord has told them they should not do? Should He do so, the Lord would be administering to sin, which is the transgression of His own law" (*The Kress Collection,* 46).

Miracles have their place, but not to the neglect of obedience or of the use of any therapy God has specified for our use.

# —— SIXTEEN ——
# The Gospel of Health Versus Fanaticism

## Miracles True and False

In the closing days of the earth, miracles done by an evil power will deceive the whole world, and will almost deceive the "elect" (see Revelation 16:14; Matthew 24:24). They will be found even within the remnant church, and often they will be miracles of *physical healing* performed in competition with health education, as will be explained later.

There are to be miracles, including healing, in the true remnant church, not in competition with health education, but in cooperation with it, in other words, health education, teaching people to obey physical law, is to have more to do with finishing the work than miracles will have to do. Satan will work miracles of healing while physical law is transgressed to cause the people to believe that obedience is not necessary. In contrast, God's healing will emphasize the necessity of obedience.

Much has been written in the Testimonies concerning this controversy between God and Satan in the closing days, revealing that this conflict will enter the remnant church and almost "deceive the elect." The most pointed of these Testimonies are reproduced here for the convenience of the reader who may not have ready access to all of them.

## Evil Angels Heal Sick

"His agents still claim to cure disease. They profess to employ electricity, magnetism, or the so-called 'sympathetic remedies'; but in truth the magnetic power of which they boast is directly attributable to the sorcery of Satan. By this means he casts his spell over the bodies and souls of men.

"The sick, the bereaved, the curious, are communicating with evil spirits. All who venture here are on dangerous ground. The Word of Truth declares how God regards them. In ancient times He pronounced judgments upon one who sent for counsel to a heathen oracle: 'Is it not because there is not a God in Israel, that ye go to inquire of Baal-zebub, the god of Ekron? Now therefore thus saith the Lord,

Thou shalt not come down from that bed on which thou art gone up, but shalt surely die' (2 Kings 1:3, 4).

"The visible and the invisible world are in close contact. Could the veil be lifted, we would see evil angels employing all their arts to deceive and destroy" (*Sketches From The Life of Paul*, 139, 140).

## Satan a Great "Medical Missionary"

"You know that Satan will come in to deceive if possible the very elect. He claims to be Christ, and he is coming in, pretending to be the great medical missionary. He will cause fire to come down from heaven in the sight of men to prove that he is God. We must stand barricaded by the truths of the Bible. The canopy of truth is the only canopy under which we can stand safely" (*Medical Ministry*, 87, 88).

## Seek to Deceive the Elect

"The time is at hand when Satan will work miracles to confirm minds in the belief that he is God. All the people of God are now to stand on the platform of truth as it has been given in the third angel's message. All the pleasant pictures, all the miracles wrought, will be presented in order that, if possible, the very elect shall be deceived. The only hope for anyone is to hold fast the evidences that have confirmed the truth in righteousness. Let these be proclaimed over and over again, until the close of earth's history" (*Review and Herald,* August 9, 1906).

## Test Satan's Miracles by Scriptures Not by Science

"The last great delusion is soon to open before us. Antichrist is to perform his marvelous works in our sight. So closely will the counterfeit resemble the true that it will be impossible to distinguish between them except by the Holy Scriptures. By their testimony every statement and every miracle must be tested" (*The Great Controversy,* 593).

## Not Trust In Miracles

"Satan is a diligent Bible student. He knows that his time is short, and he seeks at every point to counterwork the work of the Lord upon this earth. It is impossible to give any idea of the experience of the people of God who shall be alive upon the earth when celestial glory and a repetition of the persecutions of the past are blended. They will walk in the light proceeding from the throne of God. By means of the angels there will be constant communication between heaven and earth. And Satan, surrounded by evil angels, and claiming to be God, will work miracles of all kinds, to deceive, if possible, the very elect.

God's people will not find their safety in working miracles, for Satan will counterfeit the miracles that will be wrought. God's tried and tested people will find their power in the sign spoken of in Exodus 31:12–18. They are to take their stand on the Living Word, 'It is written.' This is the only foundation upon which they can stand securely. Those who have broken their covenant with God will in that day be without God and without hope" (*Testimonies, vol. 9, 16*).

## To Test Adventists

"The time will come, Christ tells us of, when many deceivers will go forth, declaring themselves to be Christ. The Saviour says, 'Go ye not after them.' We need not be deceived. Wonderful scenes, with which Satan will be closely connected, will soon take place. God's word declares that Satan will work miracles. He will make people sick, and then will suddenly remove from them his Satanic power. They will then be regarded as healed. These works of apparent healing will bring Seventh-day Adventists to the test. Many who have had great light will fail to walk in the light, because they have not become one with Christ" (*Battle Creek Letters, 6, 7*).

## Are We Prepared?

"As the curtain was lifted and I was shown the corruption of this age, my heart sickened, my spirit nearly fainted within me. I saw that the inhabitants of the earth were filling up the measure of the cup of their iniquity. God's anger is kindled and will be no more appeased until the sinners are destroyed out of the earth. Satan is Christ's personal enemy. He is the originator and leader of every species of rebellion in heaven and earth. His rage increases; we do not realize his power. If our eyes could be opened to discern the fallen angels at work with those who feel at ease and consider themselves safe, we would not feel so secure. Evil angels are upon our track every moment. We expect a readiness on the part of bad men to act as Satan suggests; but while our minds are unguarded against his invisible agents, they assume new ground and work marvels and miracles in our sight. Are we prepared to resist them by the Word of God, the only weapon we can use successfully?

"Some will be tempted to receive these wonders as from God. The sick will be healed before us. Miracles will be performed in our sight. Are we prepared for the trial which awaits us when the lying wonders of Satan shall be more fully exhibited? Will not many souls be ensnared and taken? By departing from the plain precepts and commandments of God, and giving heed to fables, the minds of many are preparing to receive these lying wonders. We must all now seek to arm ourselves for the contest in which we must soon engage. Faith in God's Word, prayerfully studied and practically applied, will be our shield from Satan's power and will bring us off conquerors through the blood of Christ" (*Testimonies*, vol. 1, 302).

## Miracles Not a Proof of True Church

"The scene of Christ's temptation was to be a lesson for all of His followers. When the enemies of Christ, by the instigation of Satan, request them to show some miracle, they should answer them as meekly as the Son of God answered Satan, 'It is said, Thou shalt not tempt the Lord thy God' (Luke 4:20). If they will not be convinced by inspired testimony, a manifestation of God's power would not benefit them. God's wondrous works are not manifested to gratify the curiosity of any. Christ, the Son of God, refused to give Satan any proof of His power. He made no effort to remove Satan's 'if,' by showing a miracle. The disciples of Christ will be brought into similar positions. Unbelievers will require them to do some miracle, if they believe God's special power is in the church, and that they are the chosen people of God. Unbelievers who are afflicted with infirmities, will require them to work a miracle upon them, if God is with them. Christ's followers should imitate the example of their Lord. Jesus, with His divine power, did not do any mighty work for Satan's diversion. Neither can the servants of Christ. They should refer the unbelieving to the written, inspired testimony for evidence of their being the loyal people of God, and heirs of salvation" (*Spiritual Gifts*, vol. 4, 150, 151).

## Satan Personates Christ

"The wrath of Satan increases as his time grows short, and his work of deceit and destruction will reach its culmination in the time of trouble.

"Fearful sights of a supernatural character will soon be revealed in the heavens, in token of the power of miracle-working demons. The spirits of devils will go forth to the kings of the earth and to the whole world, to fasten them in deception, and urge them on to unite with Satan in his last struggle against the government of heaven. By these agencies, rulers and subjects will be alike deceived. Persons will arise pretending to be Christ Himself, and claiming the title and worship which belong to the world's Redeemer. They will perform wonderful miracles of healing and will profess to have revelations from Heaven contradicting the testimony of the Scriptures.

"As the crowning act in the great drama of deception, Satan himself will personate Christ. The church has long professed to look to the Saviour's advent as the consummation of her hopes. Now the great deceiver will make it appear that Christ has come. In different parts of the earth, Satan will manifest himself among men as a majestic being of dazzling brightness, resembling the description of the Son of God given by John in the Revelation (see Revelation 1:13–15). The glory that surrounds him is unsurpassed by anything that mortal eyes have yet beheld. The shout of triumph rings out upon the air: 'Christ has come! Christ has come!' The people prostrate themselves in adoration before him, while he lifts up his hands and pronounces a blessing upon them, as Christ blessed His disciples when He was upon the earth. His voice is soft and subdued, yet full of melody. In gentle, compassionate tones he presents some of the same gracious, heavenly truths which the Saviour uttered; he heals the diseases of the people, and then, in his assumed character of Christ, he claims to have changed the Sabbath to Sunday, and commands all to hallow the day which he has blessed. He declares that those who persist in keeping holy the seventh day are blaspheming his name by refusing to listen to his angels sent to them with light, and truth. This is the strong, almost overmastering delusion. Like the Samaritans who were deceived by Simon Magus, the multitudes, from the least to the greatest, give heed to these sorceries, saying: This is 'the great power of God' [Acts 8:10]" (*The Great Controversy*, 623–625).

## A Fortunate People
Fortunate are the people to whom these terrible dangers have been revealed for their guidance through the perils of the last days. But this is not all. God has not only warned of these dangers, but He has a program to meet this situation—a program for His church to follow in perfecting their own characters, and by which to meet the enemy of mankind in his fierce battle for human souls. This is now to be studied.

## The Better Way to Work Than by Miracles
"Our success will depend on carrying forward the work in the simplicity in which Christ carried it forward.

"The way in which Christ worked was to preach the word, and to relieve suffering by miraculous works of healing. But I am instructed that we cannot now work in this way; for Satan will exercise his power by working miracles. God's servants today could not work by means of miracles, because spurious works of healing, claimed to be divine, will be wrought.

"For this reason the Lord has marked out a way in which His people are to carry forward a work of physical healing, combined with the teaching of the Word. Sanitariums are to be established, and with these institutions are to be connected workers who will carry forward genuine medical missionary work. ...

"This is the provision the Lord has made whereby gospel medical missionary work is to be done for many souls. These institutions are to be established outside the cities, and in them educational work is to be intelligently carried forward" (*Medical Ministry,* 14).

## Health Destroyers Lack Knowledge

"Some have asked me, 'Why should we have sanitariums? Why should we not, like Christ, pray for the sick, that they may be healed miraculously?' I have answered, 'Suppose we were able to do this in all cases; how many would appreciate the healing? Would those who were healed become health reformers, or continue to be health destroyers?'

"Jesus Christ is the Great Healer, but He desires that by living in conformity with His laws we may cooperate with Him in the recovery and the maintenance of health. Combined with the work of healing there must be an imparting of knowledge of how to resist temptation" (*Ibid.,* 13).

## Reformation Before Power to Heal

"After Christ's baptism He preached the gospel to the cities that were round about. He was working and healing—the medical missionary work was bound up with the preaching of the gospel. ... You may say: 'Why not then, take hold of the work, and heal the sick as Christ did?' I answer, You are not ready. Some have believed; some have been healed; but there are many who make themselves sick by intemperate eating or by indulging in other wrong habits. When they get sick, shall we pray for them to be raised up, that they may carry on the very same work again? There must be a reformation throughout our ranks; the people must reach a higher standard before we expect the power of God to be manifested in a marked manner for the healing of the sick. ... Let me tell you that the sick will be healed when you have faith to come to God in the right way' " (*General Conference Bulletin,* April 3, 1901).

## God Does Not Heal Violators

"I saw that the reason why God did not hear the prayers of His servants for the sick among us more fully was that He could not be glorified in so doing while they were violating the laws of health. And I also saw that He designed the health reform and Health Institute to prepare the way for the prayer of faith to be fully answered. Faith and good works should go hand in hand in relieving the afflicted among us, and in fitting them to glorify God here and to be saved at the coming of Christ. ...

"Let no one obtain the idea that the institute is the place for them to come to be raised up by the prayer of faith. That is the place to find relief from disease by treatment and right habits of living, and to learn how to avoid sickness. But if there is one place under the heavens more than another where soothing, sympathizing prayer should be offered by men and women of devotion and faith it is at such an institute" (*Testimonies,* vol. 1, 561).

## Sanitariums to Educate and Use No Drugs

"When the light came that we should have a sanitarium, the reason was plainly given. There were many who needed to be educated in regard to healthful living. A place must be provided to which the sick could be taken, where they could be taught how to live so as to preserve health. At the same time light was given that the sick could be successfully treated without drugs. This was the lesson that was to be practiced and taught by physicians and nurses, and by all other medical missionary workers. Drugs were to be discarded, because when they are taken into the system, their after effect is very injurious. Many suffering from fevers have died as the result of the drugs administered. They might have been alive today had they been given water treatment by those competent to administer it" (*Manuscript Releases,* vol. 7, 378).

## The Great Object to Teach

"Its great object [the sanitarium] is to teach the people how to live so as to give nature a chance to remove and resist disease" (*Testimonies,* vol. 1, 643).

## Sanitariums Exemplify True Temperance

"The world's Redeemer knew that the indulgence of appetite was bringing physical debility and deadening the perceptive faculties so that sacred and eternal things could not be discerned. He knew that self-indulgence was perverting the moral powers, and that man's great need was conversion—in heart and mind and soul, from the life of self-indulgence to one of self-denial and self-sacrifice. May the Lord help you as His servant to appeal to the ministers and to arouse the sleeping churches. Let your labors as a physician and a minister be in harmony. It is for this that our sanitariums were established, to preach the truth of true temperance" (*Counsels on Diet and Foods*, 161, 162).

## Sanitariums to Be Schools

"There should be sanitariums near all our large cities. … In these institutions men and women are to be taught how to care for their own bodies, and at the same time to become sound in the faith. … Our sanitariums are to be schools in which instruction shall be given in medical missionary lines. They are to bring to sin-sick souls the leaves of the tree of life, which will restore to them peace and hope and faith in Christ Jesus. Forbid not those who have a desire to extend this work. Let the light shine forth. All worthy health productions will create an interest in health reform. Forbid them not. The Lord would have all opportunities to extend the work taken advantage of. …

## Without Drugs

"In every large city there should be a representation of true medical missionary work The principles of genuine health reform are to be brought out in clear lines, in our health publications, and in lectures delivered to the patients in our sanitariums. In every city there are men and women who would go to a sanitarium were it near at hand, who would not be able to go to one a long way off. … It is the Lord's purpose that His method of healing without drugs shall be brought into prominence in every large city through our medical institutions. God invests with holy dignity those who go forth in His power to heal the sick. Let the light shine forth farther and still farther, in every place to which it is possible to obtain entrance. Satan will make the work as difficult as possible, but divine power will attend all true-hearted workers. Guided by our heavenly Father's hand, let us go forward" (*Medical Ministry*, 324, 325).

## Diet of Foods From the Soil

"Our sanitariums are to be the means of enlightening those who come to them for treatment. The patients are to be shown how they can live upon a diet of grains, fruits, nuts, and other products of the soil. I have been instructed that lectures should be regularly given in our sanitariums on health topics. People are to be taught to discard those articles of food that weaken the health and strength of the beings for whom Christ gave His life. …

"It is that the people may become intelligent in regard to these things that sanitariums are to be established. A great work is to be done. Those who are now ignorant are to become wise. ... People are to be taught how, by carefulness in eating and drinking, they may keep well" (*Manuscript Releases*, vol. 20, 261).

## Sanitariums Rather Than Hospitals

"The purpose of our health institutions is not first and foremost to be that of hospitals. The health institutions connected with the closing work of the gospel in the earth stand for the great principles of the gospel in all its fullness. Christ is the one to be revealed in all the institutions connected with the closing work, but none of them can do it so fully as the health institution where the sick and suffering come for relief and deliverance from both physical and spiritual ailment" (*Medical Ministry*, 27, 28).

## Surgery Not Most Important

"The study of surgery and other medical science receives much attention in the world, but the true science of medical missionary work, carried forward as Christ carried it, is new and strange to the denominational churches and to the world. But it will find its rightful place when as a people who have had great light, Seventh-day Adventists awaken to their responsibilities (*Evangelism*, 518).

## Sanitariums to Be Different

"The Lord years ago gave me special light in regard to the establishment of a health institution where the sick could be treated on altogether different lines from those followed in any other institution in our world. It was to be founded and conducted upon Bible principles, as the Lord's instrumentality, and it was to be in His hands one of the most effective agencies for giving light to the world. It was God's purpose that it should stand forth with scientific ability, with moral and spiritual power, and as a faithful sentinel of reform in all its bearings. All who should act a part in it were to be reformers, having respect to its principles, and heeding the light of health reform shining upon us as a people. ...

## In Advance of All Others

"If conducted in a manner that God could approve, it would be highly successful, and would stand in advance of all other institutions of the kind in the world" (*Testimonies*, vol. 6, 223, 224).

## Sanitariums All Over the World—
## Health Reform to Represent Adventists

"Sanitariums are to be established all through our world, and managed by a people who are in harmony with God's laws, a people who will cooperate with God in advocating the truth that determines the case of every soul for whom Christ died. ... The Lord designs that the sanitariums established among Seventh-day Adventists shall be symbols of what can be done for the world, types of the saving power of the truths of the gospel" (*Medical Ministry*, 26).

"They are to give character to the work which must be carried forward in those last days in restoring man through a reformation of the habits, appetites, and passions. Seventh-day Adventists are to be represented to the world by the advance principles of health reform which God has given us.

"Still greater truths are unfolding for this people as we draw near the close of time, and God designs that we shall everywhere establish institutions where those who are in darkness in regard to the needs of the human organism may be educated, that they in their turn may lead others into the light of health reform. The blind leaders of the blind must learn the truth in regard to healthful living as taught in the Scriptures" (*The Kress Collection*, 13).

"Plants [sanitariums] should be established in various places all over the world" (*Testimonies*, vol. 8, 204).

## Health Education Prevents Fanaticism

"Our sanitariums are to reach a class that can be reached by no other means. 'Why,' asks one and another, 'is not prayer offered for the miraculous healing of the sick, instead of so many sanitariums being established?' Should this be done, great fanaticism would arise in our ranks. ... Should we carry out the plans that some would be pleased to have us carry out, companies would be formed who would bring in spiritualistic manifestations that would confuse the faith of many.

"Errors will come in, and strange doctrines will be advocated. Some will depart from the faith, giving heed to seducing spirits and doctrines of devils. As far back as the establishment of the first sanitarium these things began to appear. They were similar to the errors that manifested themselves soon after the disappointment of 1844. A strong phase of fanaticism appeared, calling itself the witness of the Holy Ghost. I was given a message to rebuke this evil work.

"The medical missionary work is to be to the third angel's message as the right hand to the body. To be indifferent in regard to the medical missionary work is to dishonor God. The Lord would have perfect harmony prevail among His workers" (*Evangelism*, 594, 595).

"The Lord has opened this matter before me. The perverted habits of the world and the declension of religion have brought in indulgences of appetite and wrong habits of eating and drinking. The world is given over to self-indulgence and extravagance. Our sanitariums were established to educate *people* in regard to right habits of living.

"Before our first sanitarium was established, the Lord opened the plan before me, showing me that the work would be solidified if those connected with the institution were men who had genuine experience and who were fully settled in present truth" (*Testimony Studies on Diet and Foods*, 83).

"The light given me was that a sanitarium should be established, and that in it drug medication should be discarded, and simple, rational methods of treatment employed for the healing of disease. In this institution people were to be taught how to dress, breathe, and eat properly—how to prevent sickness by proper habits of living" (*Counsels on Diet and Foods*, 303).

## Health Education Is Not Fanaticism

Health education is not fanaticism, but seeking for miracles of healing while we ignore the laws of health can easily lead to a most dangerous type of fanaticism. This was stated in a Testimony quoted on this page. Great fanaticism would arise in our ranks if we abandoned the healing procedures divinely placed in the last church, and which our sanitarium system was inaugurated to promulgate in the church and in the world, namely:

1. Teaching people how to eat, dress, breathe, exercise, and rest properly;

2. The use of hydrotherapy;

3. The use of other natural means, including physiotherapy in its varied forms;

4. The use of herbs to the exclusion of all poisonous drugs;

5. Surgery when necessary.

If this sanitarium program were laid aside and prayer for the sick substituted, that would bring "fanaticism" and "spiritualistic manifestations which would confuse the faith of many."

For instance; in a church where "health reform" is not popular, the people will naturally resort to prayer when dangerous sickness comes, and plead with God to heal. This provides Satan with his opportunity to work a miracle and thus lead the one who is healed, those who engage in the prayer service, and all of the members of the church who know about the miracle, to believe it is from God when it is, in fact, from Satan. They all would be confused and deceived. Inasmuch as healing came without obedience to the laws of life, they all will conclude that *obedience is not necessary* and that is the enemy's object, to thwart obedience, loyalty. It is more important that he do this in the last church than any other place, because that church has the light which it is to bear to the whole world, and if he can keep *that church in partial darkness, he is still winning the fight.* This is not an imaginary danger, but a real one. This danger exists wherever health reform is unpopular and neglected. If it be so in every church, then this danger is universal, and it is easy enough to see the trap laid for "the very elect." If the people could know that the trap is there, they could avoid it and the danger would not exist, but, not knowing, they walk into it unawares and unwarned, to their eternal doom.

The reader is now getting only a partial knowledge of the seriousness of the situation which grows out of neglect of the gospel of health; this can go on until it becomes a state of apostasy, even though those who are in the error know it not, they "are rich and increased with goods and have need of nothing" in their own sight. How serious this matter is, the reader does not yet understand; it will be made more plain in the remaining chapters.

# SEVENTEEN

# Making "Miracles" a Substitute for Obedience to the Laws of Health

In Section 15 we have seen that if proper attention is not given to obedience to the laws of health, healing by prayer is likely to be sought by many in place of healing by obedience, and, if persisted in, may bring the power of Satan to do the miracles in answer to such prayers, and that there is danger that this will be done even by Seventh-day Adventists, and that this danger is as real and as widespread as is the unpopularity of health reform among us as a people.

## Other Phases of Christian Experience Affected

This course upsets the relation that should be maintained between faith and works in dealing with the human body and the laws of health.

The individual whose view of the relation between faith and works is unbalanced in the matter of *health so* that he looks lightly upon the importance of the observance of the laws of physiology, because he gets a miracle in answer to his prayer while violating them, will by that experience be confirmed in his view of the relation between faith and works.

When he becomes *established by a miracle* in his view of the relation between faith and works as they pertain to *health,* he will almost surely conclude that the same relation between faith and works exists in *every other phase of* Christian experience. In this way he will become established in seeking to make "the Spirit" a substitute for obedience in other phases of Christian experience, and so depart from the divine use of the seven divine means God has given to work in connection with His Spirit, as set forth in sections 1 to 10 of this treatise. In that way the Christian becomes confused concerning *every phase* of Christian experience; and note that it came from confusion over principles of healthful living.

The experience just described is not far removed from something which, in certain other churches, we frown upon as being too much of an effort to "get the Spirit" for outward demonstrations without due regard to obedience to the claims of the moral law; both experiences

119

are seeking to obtain the "gifts" of the Spirit without first experiencing the "fruits."

If a person be confused over the work of the Holy Spirit in all phases of his experience he cannot possibly succeed, and will go at last either into fanaticism or discouragement, even though he be a Seventh-day Adventist with a full knowledge of all the doctrines of God's last message. His case is hopeless because he knows not how to prepare for the coming of Christ and translation because he has turned aside from God's way of getting victory over his sins and is seeking to "climb up some other way."

This condition is *a state of apostasy* from the principles of redemption which is as serious and disastrous as raw heathenism, and even more dangerous, because the individual supposes he is a Christian, a Seventh-day Adventist—and feels safe when he has in fact been confirmed in his wrong views of Christian experience by receiving a miracle performed by a power which he knows is outside of himself, which he believed was from God when it was of Satan. This is, perhaps, the most subtle way that Satan could approach a Seventh-day Adventist to "deceive the elect."

# —— EIGHTEEN ——
## Sealed in Error

To be "sealed" means to become settled, established, and fixed to the extent that the individual will *never change*. This is not done as an arbitrary act by some power exterior to the individual, but is brought about by some experience in which the power of choice has been exercised and has reached an *eternal decision*.

Those who have gone very far in "getting the Spirit," seeking the "gifts" of the Spirit ahead of the "fruits," have had an "experience" that has settled them. They have had or seen miracles of healing or the gift of tongues, or some phenomenon exhibiting a super human power from outside of humanity which they believe to be the power of God. This phenomenon makes them feel sure that their experience in connection with the manifestation of power is right, and that therefore the teachings and form of Christian experience accompanying such phenomenon *are of God*. Thus they are held fast in that thing, and you cannot change them; they are settled, established, fixed—*sealed*—sealed in error by a miracle of healing done while the principles of healthful living were ignored. This is the purpose of Satan's miracles.

By such phenomena in the last days all the world, religious and nonreligious, will be deceived and array itself against God's truth. The falsity of such miracles cannot be detected by science, but can be tested only by the nature of the teachings accompanying them which are to be compared with the Word of God (see *The Great Controversy,* 593; *Review and Herald,* August 9, 1906).

This sealing in error can come to Seventh-day Adventists if they have some experience with a spiritualistic power working contrary to God's program, as described in the *Testimonies* given in Section 16 and 17. This is a real and grave danger now facing us as a people, and one against which the Spirit of God has already warned us in the quotations herein before given. A knowledge of and belief in doctrines will not protect us if we neglect to learn the laws of physical life God has placed within us and which we fail to observe.

# —— NINETEEN ——
# The Experience of Being Sealed by Truth

T o be sealed in truth is the same process as being sealed in error except that the person being sealed has chosen truth instead of error; he has made an *eternal decision that he will obey the truth;* he has *settled* the matter *forever.*

It is understood by most of the readers of this book that the acceptance of the Sabbath and its accompanying truths is the seal of God being applied in these last days, and that the sealing work is done by the Holy Spirit (Sealed by the Spirit, Ephesians 1:13; 4:30). Recognizing this, the section now being read will deal with the total experience of being sealed. By "Sabbath and its accompanying truths," and "total experience of being sealed" we mean the experience the Christian has with all the principles enunciated in this book beginning with "God," A Person, in the first chapter, followed by "Creation" in the second chapter. In these chapters the Sabbath was explained to be the memorial of every relation between God and man, all of which were fixed by Creation, so that the Sabbath reminds man of every duty he owes to both God and man as specified in the Ten Commandments. This makes the Sabbath the *seal of the entire law.*

## The Mark of Truth
The sealed ones are they who "receive the pure mark of truth, wrought in them by the power of the Holy Ghost" (*Testimonies,* vol. 3, 267).

## By Holy Living
"By a life of holy endeavor and firm adherence to the right the children of God were sealing their destiny" (*Ibid.,* vol. 5, 213).

## Those Who Have Decided Are Sealed
In the sealing time, "I saw a covering that God was drawing over His people to protect them in the time of trouble; and every soul that was decided on the truth and was pure in heart was to be covered with the covering of the Almighty.

"Satan knew this, and he was at work in mighty power to keep the minds of as many people as he possibly could wavering and unsettled on the truth" (*Early Writings*, 43).

In passing through the process of becoming settled or "decided on the truth," we shall have many trying experiences; among them will be the trial of having to "stand" when "the majority forsake us."

## Majority Forsake Us

"To stand in defense of truth and righteousness when the majority forsake us, to fight the battles of the Lord when champions are few, this will be our test" (*Testimonies*, vol. 5, 136).

If we are to meet successfully the test of standing alone when others forsake us, we must *know that we are right,* that our experience is sound, and must have made up our minds that we will *never turn back.* In the darkness of trial we shall be held to our course by *experiences* we have had all along the way up to that time.

## Past Experience Should Guide

"Oh, for a living, active faith! We need it; we must have it, or we shall faint and fail in the day of trial. The darkness that will then rest upon our path must not discourage us or drive us to despair. It is the veil with which God covers His glory when He comes to impart rich blessings. We should know this by our past experience. In that day when God has a controversy with His people this experience will be a source of comfort and hope" (*Ibid.*, 215).

Therefore God has planned that things shall come into *our experience* that will *confirm* and *establish us* so thoroughly that *no storm, no darkness, no trial, no coldness, worldliness or apostasy of others,* can cause us to waver in the least. What would such experience be?

## Our Own Experience

It is our own heart's experience which holds us in line and keeps us going heavenward. If a man *doubt his own experience,* or if he is not sure he is having a right or sound experience, he is like a ship *without a rudder. This is* of the utmost importance. It is one thing to *know a* truth, but quite another thing to know for sure that it is the truth and be so sure that nothing can move you from it.

The greatest achievement in Christian experience is not only to have a right experience, but to be so absolutely certain that it is a right experience that no influence can cause you to doubt it or lead you into confusion; then you are *sure to go through.* Otherwise, something may arise that will lead you in another direction.

Therefore there must come into our experience things which will assure, convince, confirm and settle us in the absolute conviction that we have the truth, and that we are experiencing the truth, so that nothing can discourage us or bring us into despair or cause us to turn back or waver. Then we will *go through to the end.*

## A Lesson from Christ

Jesus went through this experience while a Son of Man on this earth. Christ on the cross in the crisis of His life "relied upon the evidence of His Father's acceptance *heretofore* given Him" (*The Desire of Ages*, 756).

He did not know that He was the Son of God until He was 12 years of age (see *The Desire of Ages*, 78; Luke 2:42–50).

All through the Saviour's life Satan worked to cause Him to doubt the Word of God and to doubt His *own experience* as being in harmony with and fulfilling that Word. In the wilderness of temptation he came as an angel of light and raised a question about Jesus' really being the Son of God. He told Jesus that "one of the most powerful of the angels … has been banished from heaven," and that Jesus' appearance and circumstances indicated that He was that fallen angel, forsaken of God and deserted by man. "If thou be the Son of God command this stone that it be made bread." Such an act would end the controversy (see *The Desire of Ages*, 118, 119).

However, Jesus remembered His own experience under the Word of God at His baptism when His Father's voice had spoken from heaven saying, "This is my Son in whom I am well pleased" (Matthew 3:17), and again on the mount of transfiguration (Matthew 17:5), the same miracle of words had been repeated to Him.

All through His life He was having experiences which confirmed Him in the belief of who He was and what His mission was, and that He was fulfilling that mission in harmony with the Word of God.

These experiences came from a power which He recognized as being from without Himself.

Throughout His life He was working miracles of all kinds by a power which He recognized rested upon Him from God.

All of these things are included in the "evidences heretofore given Him," and these experiences had so thoroughly established Him that He could not be shaken or caused to waver; and they held Him.

## Evidences of the Past Held Him

"Amid the awful darkness, apparently forsaken of God, Christ had drained the last dregs in the cup of human woe. In those dreadful hours He had relied upon the evidence of His Father's acceptance heretofore given Him. He was acquainted with the character of His Father; He understood His justice, His mercy, and His great love. By faith He rested in Him whom it had ever been His joy to obey. And as in submission He committed Himself to God, the sense of the loss of His Father's favor was withdrawn. By faith, Christ was victor (*Ibid.*, 756).

So with us. Our past should be dotted with experiences where we *know* we had the light, and know that we were *walking in* it—that the experience we had *was of God;* we must be so sure of it that we will not ever turn back.

## John the Baptist

John the Baptist almost yielded to discouragement and doubt while languishing in prison. He had preached Christ and introduced Him to the world as "the Lamb of God, which taketh away the sin of the world" (John 1:29). But Jesus did nothing for him when he was seized and put in prison. Apparently, Jesus had forgotten him and ignored him. So John wondered whether or not his own message had been right. His *message* was born of his own experience, they were inseparable; if one was wrong the other was also wrong. Therefore one day he sent his disciples to Jesus to ask Him plainly, "Art Thou He that should come or do we look for another?" (Matthew 11:4). Jesus settled him by reports of His *miracles.* John was confirmed and settled in his experience by something done by a superhuman power.

## Lessons from the Experiences of Ellen G. White

Some very valuable lessons have been learned by the author of this book from the recorded experiences of Mrs. White. Some of these records are introduced here with the hope that the reader may be likewise blessed.

Let it be remembered that we are settled, decided, and sealed in either truth or error, and that we are helped to a decision by having or knowing about some experience which came through the operation of some superhuman power. If the power was evil, associated with it were teachings contradicting the Word of God. If we do not examine the teachings and compare them with the Word of God, we will almost surely accept the manifestation of power to be of God and so be deceived concerning the false teaching. However, if we do examine the teachings associated with the supernatural power and find them to be the Word of God, then the presence of a miraculous power is added proof to us that the power is of God. The working of supernatural power has a part to act in our becoming settled and sealed, but it is not necessary for us to yield to the wrong power, because an examination of the accompanying teachings will reveal which kind of power is present. With these principles in mind, we will study the life of Ellen G. White.

A few glimpses into her inner heart's experience are gleaned from her various writings:

## "I know," " I SHALL NEVER WAVER"

"I believe in God. I know in whom I believe. I believe the messages that God has given to His remnant church. From childhood I have had many, many experiences that have strengthened my faith in the work that God has given me to do. ...

"In the early days of the message, when our numbers were few, we studied diligently to understand the meaning of many Scriptures. At times it seemed as if no explanation could be given. My mind seemed to be locked to an understanding of the Word; but when our brethren who had assembled for study, came to a point where they could go no farther, and had recourse to earnest prayer, the Spirit of God would rest upon me, and I would be taken off in vision, and be instructed in regard to the relation of scripture to scripture. These experiences were repeated over and over and over again. Thus many truths of the third angel's messages were established, point by point. Think you that my faith in this message will ever waver? Think you that I can remain silent, when I see an effort being made to sweep away the foundation pillars of our faith? I am as thoroughly established in these truths as it is possible for a person to be. I can never forget the experience I have passed through. God has confirmed my belief by many evidences of His power. ...

"I thank God that He has preserved my voice, which in my early youth physicians and friends declared would be silent within three months. The God of heaven saw that I needed to pass through a trying experience in order to be prepared for the work He had for me to do. For the past half century my faith in the ultimate triumph of the third angel's message and everything connected with it, has been substantiated by the wonderful experiences through which I have passed" (*Review and Herald,* June 14, 1906).

"We have our experience, attested to by the miraculous working of the Holy Spirit" (*Selected Messages,* book 1, 205).

"The truth ... point by point, has been sought out by prayerful study, and testified to by the miracle-working power of the Lord" (*Ibid.,* 208).

"We must know that we have not followed cunningly devised fables. Our Father bids us call to mind the former days, after which, when we were illumined, we endured a great fight of affliction. I have received most precious assurances that our early experiences were of God. I wish that every one of our people might know, as I know, of the sure and certain way in which the Lord led us in times past" (*Medical Ministry*, 102, 103).

## What Lessons from Her May Do for Others

In the midst of the article quoted above from *Review and Herald* of June 14, 1906, is this statement:

"These messages were thus given to substantiate the faith of all, that in these last days we might have confidence in the Spirit of Prophecy."

In other words, every miraculous thing which occurred in her seventy-one years of public ministry helped to convince *her* of the divinity of her work. Likewise, all those who know of her experiences can receive a similar conviction without each person having some phenomenon in his own life.

However, it does not stop here. In addition to this, we as individuals have special experiences of our own in the truth, in receiving special blessings at times, special guidance for certain occasions and needs in special answers to our prayers, by providences which come to us as individuals, and sometimes by miracles, and many wonderful experiences under the latter rain, all of which singly and collectively operate to *confirm, establish, settle,* and *seal us* in the truth.

## Never Change

This work is to go on until we reach the place where we have become so decided, so determined, so settled, so fixed, that we *will never change* though all others apostatize and we stand alone; so fixed that false miracles, derision, persecution, and even death itself *cannot move* us. Then it is that God can say, "They are now ready, I will take them. It is now safe to transplant them into heaven." Moreover, when He gets a *church* composed of people who have gone that far in their experiences, *that will finish His work, and He will come.*

## Character Perfected

"When the character of Christ shall be perfectly reproduced in His people, then He will come to claim them as His own" (*Christ's Object Lessons*, 69).

## Then the End Will Come

"Every character will be fully developed; and all will show whether they have chosen the side of loyalty or that of rebellion. Then the end will come" (*The Desire of Ages,* 763).

"The God of all grace, who hath called us unto his eternal glory by Christ Jesus, after that ye have suffered a while, make you perfect, stablish, strengthen, settle you" (1 Peter 5:10).

## Heavenly Light Floods Our Homeward Way

It is hoped that the reader has received enough help from this book so that he knows exactly how to proceed in his experience to be saved.

If we have a great task to perform, and do not know how to attack it, or how to proceed with it, our case is hopeless; but, even though the task be great, if we know exactly how to go about it, and how to continue until it is finished, so that every step in life's journey is one step nearer "home," then the heart is light and full of courage, and every day is one of delight, advancement and victory, and happy anticipation of ultimate triumph at the journey's end. That this may be the experience of every reader is the purpose of these chapters.